MW01700250

About The Author

Not long after she graduated from Engineering Graphics Technology at the Southern Alberta Institute of Technology in Calgary, Alberta, Susan Fraser discovered that drafting for a living left her too little time for her foremost interest—art. She then began alternating periods of drafting with periods of painting. The paintings she produced during her spells of intense artistic activity she exhibited in Lethbridge, Calgary and Edmonton. All her exhibits have been largely concerned with ideas and human behavior and have been somewhat narrative in nature. She is much interested in science and philosophy and in the role religion plays in our lives. Finding drawings and paintings alone to be too vague and limiting a means by which to deal artistically with those things that deeply interest her, she turned to the Canada Council Explorations Program for financial assistance in developing a more specific and comprehensive means of dealing with her subject matter. *Everything and Nothing* is the result of that appeal and the subsequent employment of the Canada Council's assistance in the realization of her aim.

Everything and Nothing

Everything and Nothing

(a play on words, numbers, and pictures)

Susan Fraser

VPG
virtual publishing group, inc.

ISBN # 1-930916-48-5

Information Address:
Virtual Publishing Group, Inc.
2817 Stanton Street,
Berkeley, California 94702-2522
U.S.A.
Published and Printed in the United States of America

To Mom and Dad,
who taught me the power of appreciation

I wish to thank the
Canada Council Explorations Program
for its funding assistance in the realization of this work.

The Canada Council for the Arts | Le Conseil des Arts du Canada

Contents

Have you got what it takes to go no place
and leave it all behind—
to be and not to be
in a disembodied mind? . . .

One

[*One's eyes open.*] Darkness. What time is it? I wonder.

[*Sits up.*] What the— ?!

[*Eyes wide, looking around.*] Wh-where am I?! What is this place?!

[*Stands up.*]

[*Looks around and around and around.*] I can't believe what I'm seeing—nothing. Nothing but black and white.

[*The line between the two extremes begins to undulate. One is getting dizzy.*]

[*Stops turning. Teeters slightly. Puts fingers to temples to steady thoughts.*]

I'm surrounded by a continuous wall of black and white. It appears I'm in a cylinder of some sort, a cylinder with a black and white interior.

That must be it. That must be where I am. But how did I get here? And why am I here? [*Raises voice.*] Hello? Is there anyone out there? Hello?

[*Waits, listens.*] Nothing. My voice sounded so flat too, like it had all the depth wrung out of it. Wherever I am, it certainly doesn't resonate with my presence. I don't even cast so much as a shadow.

I wonder what that wall feels like. It certainly is black and it certainly is white.

[*Walks and reaches for wall.*]

[*Still walking and reaching for wall.*] Now that's odd. Very odd. The wall looks so close, yet I can't touch anything. Either the wall moves as I move or it's a lot farther away than it looks.

[*Still walking, still reaching.*]

[*Still walking as arm falls lower and lower.*]

[*Stops, turns around and looks back.*] Same as before. Exactly. I don't appear to have moved in the least.

How do I get out of here if I can't even reach the wall? [*Looks down.*] Through the floor? [*Stamps around.*] Solid, by the sound and feel of it—by the look of it too. Not even so much as a seam to be seen anywhere. Big too. Stretching for as far as the eye can see—white, that is.

I wonder.

No, couldn't be. That black is too black to be as far away as that, and the white too white.

Still, one has to wonder. Plane or plain? Escarp or sky? Could that line between black and white be the join between two perpendicular surfaces? The one a cylindrical, black wall and the other a circular, white floor? It would have to be an awful big cylinder then. A sort of world in itself, though not much of one.

[*Looks up uneasily at the heavy blackness directly overhead.*] For all the room there might actually be here, this is certainly an oppressive place. One moment I feel walled in tight all round and the next I feel I'm being squeezed between two planes, one black, the other white.

I know one thing for certain. I've got to get out of here—and soon. I'll lose my mind if I don't. But how? Walking doesn't seem to help, and yelling doesn't seem to do any good either. Apparently, sound travels no better here than I do. Still, I can't just stand here.

That's it then. I've got to move on. That's all I can do.

It doesn't seem to matter what direction I take. Nor do I know anymore which direction I was going in or which I came from. So I

I’m surrounded by a continuous wall of black and white.

might as well start walking in the direction I'm already pointed. [*Starts walking.*] I only hope I don't end up walking in circles. Where there's nothing but nothing to take one's bearings from, I should think that all too possible.

If I could just reach a wall, surely I could follow it around till I came to a door.

[*Walking.*]

[*Walking.*]

[*Walking.*]

[*Walking.*]

[*Walking.*] How long must I go on like this? How far?

[*Stops. Looks around.*] This is ridiculous. I'm not getting anywhere—nowhere that I can see. And this place is beginning to bother my eyes as well as my mind. But then, from the looks of things, I could walk around here endlessly with my eyes closed and never run into or trip over anything. [*Closes eyes.*] I can't take much more of this. [*Rubs eyes.*] I don't know what I'm going to do if I don't see something soon. [*Opens eyes and blinks to focus.*] Same old, same old. No, wait! I didn't see that before: a tiny flaw in that otherwise perfectly straight line! What is it? What does it mean? I've got to find out.

[*Walking.*] I'm afraid to blink lest I lose sight of it.

[*Walking.*]

[*Walking.*] It's getting larger! It is something!

[*Faster.*]

[*Faster.*]

[*Running.*]

[*Running.*]

What the— ?

[*Slows to a walk.*]

A signpost?

[*Standing before signpost.*]

[*Flying in the air!*]

[*Crashing backwards to the ground!*]

A signpost?

Two

Foremost Figure: Oooo, look what we have here. Oh, please don't get up on our account.

One: Wh-who are you?

FF: Can't you count?

O: C-count?

FF: Yes, we are as many as we are. We are Nine.

O: Nine?

FF: Yes, Nine. I'm Two, Three's behind the Two of me, and the Four in back is Four.

O: You have numbers for names?

FF (Two): That surprises you?

O: Y-yes, it does.

Two: It shouldn't. If we can have names for numbers, we can certainly have numbers for names.

O: I-I guess so. I've just never met anyone with a number for a name before.

Oooo, look what we have here.

T: Then you haven't met much. Furthermore, we are not One. We are Nine. You are One.

O: One what?

T: Just One. Your first and last names are One and the same.

O: My name isn't One. I have a name for a name, not a number. It's—

T: One.

O: It is not.

T: It is. It's every One's name here.

O: Then why aren't any of you named One?

T: Because there are Two, Three and Four of us—Nine of us—instead of One.

O: But there aren't really nine of you. There are only three.

T: You can see only Three of us?

O: Of course I can see only three of you.

T: Then you can see right through the first Two, but you can't see past Three.

O: What's that supposed to mean: that Three is all I can see? Well, I'll have you know I can see more than Three. I can see the other two of you too—better even than I can see Three, because it keeps ducking behind you, Two.

T: Then you see Five of us now, instead of Three.

O: No, I don't see five of you either. [*Points directly at each figure in succession.*] I see three: one, two, three. See?

T: I see you see Six of us now and you've forgotten our names already.

Three: [*timidly*] Th-they say some Ones aren't good at all at remembering names; they're better at remembering numbers. And some Ones are worse at remembering numbers than names.

T: [*indignantly*] They say that, do they?

Three: Y-yes, th-they do.

T: And what do they say about Ones like this One, Ones who don't seem to be able to remember either?

Three: I-I don't know.

T: You don't know?!

Three: N-no, I-I don't.

T: Then you shouldn't have said anything. Nothing you had to say had anything to with the One we're speaking to. And besides, you're speaking out of turn. The Three of you are third, after the Two of me. And I'm not done speaking yet. So— [*Grabs at something behind Three's head and pulls.*] —ssshhhush, will you!

O: [*Moves to stand.*] Nor am I done speaking, and I'm One—first, according to you. [*Falls back again with a push from Two.*] Hey! What do you think you're doing?!

T: Pushing you down again. We asked you not to get up on our account.

O: It's on your account I'm down here: shooting up under me the way you did, knocking me off my feet.

T: When we first surfaced, you mean?

O: Surfaced! That's putting it mildly. I thought the ground had exploded under me. What's with you anyway? From the looks of you, you still haven't completely surfaced. Why does the surface of this place go up over you like that? Are you part of this place or something?

T: Both.

O: Both? What do you mean "both"?

T: We are both part of this place and something.

O: Something? Where did that come from?

T: You asked us if we were part of this place or something.

O: By "something" I meant some such thing, though. At least I think I did. I know I didn't mean to ask you if you were something. It's obvious to me you are. I can see you plain enough. I just don't know what to make of you. What exactly are you anyway?

T: What we are exactly is of no consequence whatsoever. What's really important is that we are something.

O: I don't see what's so important about that. Everything's something of some sort or another.

T: Not here. Here a thing is only something if it's not nothing, only if it means more. If it doesn't mean more, then it's nothing and not something.

O: But you just said that what you are is of no consequence. How can what you are be of no consequence and you still be important?—if that's what you mean by meaning more. Or do you

So ssshhhush, will you!

mean "more" in the purely quantitative sense? There are more of you than there are of me, that sort of thing? Enough to make you feel free to knock me down.

T: That was your doing, not ours.

O: That's what I get for standing where I did just then, you mean?

T: Well, you did stand just there.

O: Maybe so, but I'm not standing—or sitting rather—for any more of this. [*Moves to rise.*]

T: [*Presses down on One's shoulder.*] Oh, but you don't *really* want to get up just yet.

O: What do you know about what I really want?

T: Everything.

O: How—

T: You wouldn't be this far if you didn't.

O: This far? I'm nowhere at all.

T: Not quite. But just about.

O: What makes you think I want to be nowhere at all?

T: You do want to get out of here, don't you?

O: Yes, but *this* is nowhere.

T: Not quite. Very nearly, though.

O: Why do I get the feeling this conversation is going in circles—nowhere, in other words?

T: Because you are?

O: No, because I'm going crazy and you're driving me there—you and that ridiculous signpost.

T: Ah yes, the signpost. That's there to give One any directions It might want.

O: Directions? All it does is point all over the place.

T: In all sorts of directions.

O: But it doesn't say anything about them. Not on any one of all those different directions does it say what thing or place is to be found in that direction. It's the most pointless, pointy signpost I've ever seen.

T: The signpost is nothing at all to you then? Its existence is of no consequence whatsoever to you? It may as well not be as be, for all the difference it makes to you?

O: I don't know that I'd go that far. Not when I consider how much it meant to me when I first caught the barest glimpse of it on the horizon. That is the horizon, isn't it—that line between black and white?

T: What else could it be?

O: Yes, well, anyway, that signpost was everything to me when I first caught the slightest sight of it. I even started running toward it. And what a moving experience that was.

T: Running toward the signpost?

O: Oh yes, it felt so good to feel like I was moving again. I've never been anywhere that made me feel so much like I was going nowhere wherever I went there as this place. The land here is so flat and the land and sky so void of detail there's nothing whatsoever for one to take one's bearings from. Nothing to move toward or away from or to the right or left of, nothing to go around or over or under—except the land and the sky of course.

T: But is not the going easiest and speediest where things are flattest? Can One not go the greatest distance in any direction in the least amount of time with the least amount of effort where things are absolutely flat? Can One not move flat out through such a world?

O: What is the good of going the greatest distance in any direction in the least amount of time with the least amount of effort, if one never has any sensation of going or getting anywhere? And if, in going the distance, one only becomes more and more numb from the utter sameness of it all? What good are ease and speed then? They're good for driving one mad, that's what they're good for. I know. I was on the verge of losing my mind when I caught the tiniest hint of the signpost up ahead of me. It was such a welcome change to the flatness of it all that I quite forgot about losing my mind and started fearing I'd lost the signpost.

T: The signpost saved you from losing your mind then?

O: Till I got close enough to it to see fully what it was. When I saw the signs on it were as blank as the landscape, I went back to thinking I was going to lose my mind—till you three shot up under me and knocked more than my mind off track.

T: We took your mind off your mind then.

O: Completely.

T: Good of us, wasn't it?

O: Good of you? It was downright rude of you.

T: But did we not save you from losing your mind by causing you to forget about losing it?

O: In a most inconsiderate manner—before you tried to make me lose it once and for all with all your nonsense about names and numbers. And that business about being something and meaning more. You still haven't explained that. You're not going to tell me, are you, that the reason you mean more is the extreme scarcity of things around here? Where there's nothing, anything is bound to mean something—everything even. If that's the case, if that's how there's more to you than can be accounted for by simply counting your number, then how much would Three be worth if it was the only one here? Would it still rate a Nine? Or would it rate a still higher rating? Would it be *really* something then?

T: Three could never be the only One here because Three is not One. It is Three. So wherever Three is, Three are.

O: There, you see. You used "is" instead of using "are" twice. And you used "it" instead of "they" to refer to Three. You don't see Three as three separate entities any more than I do. You know full well Three is just the name of one of you.

T: There is no One among us. You are the only One here.

O: Oh, so now there are none of you instead of nine. So I'm the only one here now. From nine to none, just like that. From an "i" to an "o" and "Poof!" you're zero. Two can play your game, Two. Or should I say Three—you and me? Or how about Ten—all Ten of the four of us? [*Attempts again to rise.*]

T: [*Shoves One down again.*] Just because you can't count properly—

O: Oh, I can count all right, good and proper too. What I can't do is stand up. Why do you insist on pushing me down every time I try to get up? Is it because I don't count as well as can't count?

T: If you really thought that we would be calling you No-one instead of One, or None for short. Or perhaps we would see you as having a capital zero instead of a capital "O" at the beginning of your name—if we could see you, that is. It's very difficult to see nothing.

O: Three, though—that's as easy as Nine to see. I don't know what makes you believe you can make more of yourselves simply by calling yourselves numbers greater than your actual number.

And why stop at Two, Three and Four? You could have made a whole lot more of yourselves just by calling yourselves Twenty, Thirty and Forty, or by tacking a surname like Hundred, Thousand or Million onto the numbers you go by. It would have been so fast and easy to be so much more than you've settled for.

T: You do agree, then, that ease and speed are essential to greatness, especially a greatness of considerable quantity.

O: I don't know if I do or not. It depends what you mean by greatness. To me there's a lot more to more than pure quantity—than just numbers. It not only takes more to materialize more of anything than simply assigning it a higher number, it takes more than just more of anything to make it mean more, importance-wise. Not even things in great plenitude can have much, if any, significance—certainly none beyond that which they can achieve by sheer force of number—if they cannot make some sort of significant difference, if they cannot make things better or worse by being there. Of course, a positive difference is always preferable to a negative one. Things that add value to life make the world a better place by being there, and better and better the greater the numbers they exist in—to a point anyway.

T: And things of that sort—somethings, that is—cannot be realized by One in considerable quantities without the power to realize them with considerable ease and speed.

O: That's true, yes. So that's what you mean by somethings or things that mean more. You mean things that add to one's life or that help one's life mean more to it. But you said your little threesome of Nine was something, and you haven't done anything for me. To me, yes, but not for me. You've done nothing but put me down and keep me down for the count. Still, if you would only tell me how to get out of here, I would think the world of you.

T: That's what we're here for.

O: It is? Why am I here?

T: Why, to get out of here of course.

O: And you're here to tell me how.

T: Insofar as you can tell yourself how.

O: What?

T: You're "It," you see—It with a capital "I" before the "t." You're what It's all about. You're Everything here—or very nearly. Every One is who has got this far.

O: But I don't understand. Can't you be a little clearer than that?

T: We can be as clear as you want us to be, even clear enough to be seen right through.

O: Then be so, please.

T: Right. But first we've got this to say. [*Turns to look at Four.*] How about it, Four? Have you your box ready?

[*Four shows the first signs of being more than just a stone statue by pulling a box out of seeming nowhere and taking and eating popcorn from it.*]

T: Good. We're set then. [*Turns back to face One, takes a deep breath and begins:*]

While the Four of us eat popcorn
The popcorn box eats naught,
Eating just as much as Four,
Though what it eats is not.
Which leaves only the Five of us
To do as we must do
To leave One even more nonplussed
And minused from us too.

Yes, one is an odd number—
An even odder One to be.
Enough to make One wonder
Why It ever came to be.
But only till It realize
The more of which It dreams
And realize there's more to life
Than mere existence means.

Still, more is not the most there is
Or even that can be,
So long as there is less to give
And more to get for free,

As One Itself must be aware
To have come so far from here
To realize Its greatest share
By that mighty means most mere.

As for any other Its
One might meet along the way
As It seeks the means of exit
By which to leave and stay,
Every One's a One like It
With an End which is the same
And has stayed and gone as far as It
To realize that Aim.

As the One and Only head-liner,
The star of this here show,
The One with all the One-liners
To play the leading role,
You have front and center seat to see
Just how to count quite properly—
Or that special means by which to be
The One to count quite utterly.

Now, not to put too fine a point
On the sign we're giving you
Of just how much we've all enjoyed
Our meeting up with you,
We offer up these numbers
To provide you with a clue
That will ease your sense of wonder
As to where you're froming to.

Add three of Nine to one of One
To get a sum of four of Ten.
Then take three of Nine from the sum
To make the start equal the end.

Two

That leaves One free to wander round
From here to here and back again,
Where things start off at where they're bound
And One plus Zero equals Ten.

And so with that we've said our piece
And must count down from Ten,
If we are to make ourselves the least
And leave you now as then.

10,
9,
8,
7,
6,
5,
4,
3,
2,
1.

O: [*Scrambles to feet.*] Hey! Wait! You're not supposed to leave! Not yet! You haven't told me how to get out of here! Stop! Stop! [*Pounces on the top of Four's disappearing head. Nothing—but the bone-jarring response of a ground gone as hard and flat as before.*] Well, I never— ! Talk about rude! That hurt too—the ground turning on me like that.

Well, what am I supposed to do now? Just sit here? I doubt that, despite what Two said, whatever that was exactly. I want out of here, and I don't imagine I'll get out without finding some way out. Those three were no help to me. I'm going to have to do it myself. But how? [*Spies abandoned box on ground, crawls over to it, picks it up and examines it.*] Nothing in it. Something on it, though.

Now would be a good time to start seeing things—
like a box, for instance.

10, 9, 8, 7, 6, 5, 4, 3, 2, 1.

Ha! Is that supposed to be funny? If it is, it isn't. [*Tosses box aside, leans back against signpost and stares vacantly into the vacant distance.*]

[*Suddenly sees something—again something ever so small barely pricking the blackness directly ahead.*] I wonder what it is this time. Not another pointless signpost I hope. [*Stands and scans the horizon all round, looking for anything else previously missed. Nothing. Not even the tiny spur of white.*] Oh no, I've lost it! No, there it is! Thank heavens!

Well, here I go. I'm only glad I don't have to strike out alone from the signpost, with not so much as anything to head for. I don't know that I could have left the maddening thing behind otherwise. [*Starts walking.*]

[*Breaks into a jog.*]

[*Jogging.*]

[*Jogging.*]

[*Jogging.*]

[*Jogging.*]

[*Still jogging with eyes straight ahead.*] Well, at least it's not shaping up to be another signpost. More like a . . .

Three

. . . box. A big one too by the looks of it. A building maybe.

[*Standing before a box the size of a house with the proportions more of a popcorn box than of a house. Hearing muffled voices from inside the box.*] I wonder who's inside. Some more Ones? There are supposed to be other Ones here, according to Two. Other Its, as Two put it. I hope they can be of more help to me than those last three or Nine or whatever were. I wonder what they're talking about in there. I can't make it out, whatever it is. [*Walks round to the end of the box where two great, cardboard flaps stand guard, door-like, before the entrance.*] A standoffish sort of box from the looks of it. Still, I do want to know how to get out of here. And I am curious to know what's going on in there. So— [*Pauses a moment to gather courage.*] —here goes nothing. [*Knocks on one of the flaps.*] Hello in there!

First Voice: [*loud with surprise*] There's some One at the doors!

Second Voice: There can't be! We didn't invite any One to the party!

One: [*Straining to hear and be heard.*] Pardon me, but did you say party? Is there a party going on in there?

SV: A tea party, yes.

FV: And it's all for Nothing.

O: Oh, I'm sorry to hear that.

FV: Why?

O: Because it must be very disappointing for you.

FV: What?

O: The party.

FV: Why?

O: Because it turned out to be all for nothing.

SV: Why should we be disappointed that the party turned out to be just the party we planned it to be?

O: You wanted the party to end up being all for nothing?

FV: We most certainly did.

O: Why?

SV: If you have to ask that, you don't know Nothing.

O: I hope not. Or rather, I hope so. That is, I hope I don't know nothing.

SV: What's that? You've no desire to know Nothing?

O: Of course not.

FV: Then you'd better go.

O: Go where?

FV: Go away.

O: Why? Because I have no desire to know nothing?

SV: We were thinking of giving you a chance to know Nothing better by bending the party rules a bit and letting you join the party. But as you've no desire to know Nothing, you're only wasting our time and yours poking your voice into a party you have no desire to join.

O: [*Looks round at the inscrutable scenery.*] As I can't see how I could know any less than I do right now, I may as well join the party.

FV: What's that? What did you just say?

O: Oh, I was just talking to myself. That's all. And I changed my mind. I do want to know nothing better. I do want to be part of your party.

FV: Talked some sense into yourself, did you?

SV: Come in, come in then. Let yourself in.

O: I can't. I can't open either of the doors. There's no handle on either of them.

SV: Yes, to keep any One from coming to our party. We'll have to come and let you in then.

O: [*Hears footsteps. Watches as the doors swing outward to reveal a very large rabbit and an individual in a top hat and suit. Notices that both characters sport zippers that begin at their waists and run up the centre of their torsos to their chins. Thinks, "Now that's odd. The zipper on the One with the hat goes all the way up the middle of Its face."*]

FV (Rabbit): So that's the face behind the voice at the door.

O: So that's the mask behind the first voice I heard.

SV (Zipper Face): Yes, we can see you, but you can't see us.

O: I can see you, but I can't see *you.*

Zipper Face: Wonderfully mysterious, isn't it?

O: For you maybe.

ZF: Come, come, join the party. [*Motions to One to follow It and the other into the box.*]

O: [*Steps hurriedly into the box as the doors swing shut again. Sees a rectangular section of white floor, in the middle of which stands a rectangular table covered with a white, floor-length tablecloth and a heap of empty bottles, boxes, bags and cans. Notices that the height of the box is utterly lost in the absolute blackness of its walls and ceiling. Watches as the other two seat themselves atop two smaller, white boxes at the far end of the table where three cups, three saucers and a teapot sit in a small clearing. Moves to select a box seat from the other white boxes scattered here and there about the table.*]

ZF: We hope you don't mind, but we prefer that you sit some distance down the table from us, till we see what sort of table manners you have.

O: [*Thinks, "Manners?! From the looks of the table, you're hardly One to judge another's table manners." Takes a deep breath. "Oh well, no point in getting thrown out no sooner than I've been invited in." Selects a box and sits somewhat apart from the other two.*]

Rabbit: [*Seizes teapot, tips it upside down and shakes it angrily.*]

ZF: Oh, you'll have to excuse the hare here.

O: Hare? I thought It was a rabbit.

ZF: Oh no. It's much too big to be a rabbit. Hares are usually bigger than rabbits, you know.

O: Maybe so, but isn't It too big to be a hare too?

ZF: Be careful what you say. The hare went to a lot of trouble to look like a hare, so It's not likely to take too kindly to any such criticism of It. Lucky for you, It was too busy to hear what you said.

O: What's It doing anyway?

ZF: It's attempting to have some tea.

O: It is?

ZF: And the tea is being difficult of course. It usually is at parties like this one.

O: Tea parties, you mean?

ZF: Parties for Nothing, actually.

O: Are there many such parties?

ZF: Oh yes, and we three go to all of them.

O: You three? I see only two of you.

ZF: Oh, that's right. You haven't seen the third member of our little party of partiers yet. [*Glances down at the floor, looks up at the hare.*]

Hare. Oh, hare. You know how I hate to interrupt you when you're pouring yourself a cup of tea, but you are the closest to It. Would you be a sport and pick It up so I can show It to this One here?

R (Hare): [*Grumbles something, slams the teapot down on the table, leans sideways and slowly sits up again with a large, sleepy mouse in tow. Plunks the mouse down on a nearby box and returns to Its struggle with the tea, while the listless mouse slumps forward and tumbles slowly back to the floor.*]

ZF: There, you see—three.

O: Yes, I see. That's one tired mouse.

ZF: Quite partied out.

O: And all for nothing too—if this party is all for nothing.

ZF: Which it most certainly is. Capital stuff, Nothing. Deserving of a capital "N," if anything is.

There, you see—three.

O: I'm afraid I don't see how nothing could mean anything to any One.

ZF: Then I'll have to show you how. But first I think I should clear the table so I can show you more clearly. [*Coolly sweeps the two cups and saucers nearest It from the table to the floor. Reaches over the table and sweeps the litter of boxes, bottles, bags, and cans to the floor as well.*]

O: [*Assists by brushing the litter from the opposite side of the table.*]

ZF: [*Removes hat, places it on the table, stands and leans forward over the table.*]

O: Wh-wha— What happened?! What's wrong with your head?!

ZF: Nothing that a little more Nothing wouldn't cure.

O: What do you mean? There's not enough space for your head?

ZF: Does it not look that way?

O: What happened to the space? The ceiling hasn't fallen, has it?! [*Moves to stand.*]

ZF: Oh don't get up. You'll only bring it down on you that much faster.

O: What?! The ceiling is falling?!

ZF: [*Calmly sits down and restores Its head and hat to their previous states.*]

O: Shouldn't we be getting out of here?!

ZF: That would be leaving the party.

O: There won't be any party if the ceiling hits the floor!

ZF: Oh, it won't do that. In fact, the ceiling's no lower than it ever was. I merely made it look lower to show you what things would be like if there was not enough Nothing about. Things would be somewhat out of shape, wouldn't they?

O: If they weren't squashed right out of existence.

ZF: So you see now how Nothing can be something to One—everything even, when in very short supply.

O: I guess so. But I don't see why any One would throw a party for Nothing.

ZF: Why, it's the least any One can do to honour the least, considering the room it makes for every One and everything else in the world.

What's wrong with your head?!

O: But if there wasn't anything worthwhile in the world to fill the room it made there, then Nothing would mean nothing. It wouldn't mean anything.

ZF: Ah, but it's because of Nothing that there are so many somethings in the world. More and more good things all the time, in fact.

O: I don't see how Nothing can be responsible for the growing number of good things there are in the world.

ZF: Then I shall have to tell you how. And to do that I will tell you a tale, a tale about an experience I had. It goes like this:

One night I threw a party—so hard it disappeared.
And when the guests were gone something happened, something weird.
I was sitting in my easy chair talking to my tea
About Nothing in particular—that is, Naught especially—
When on a sudden I remembered I was very short of funds.
In fact my pockets were so empty I might as well've had none.
It was then I started looking 'neath the pillow in my chair
For any easy money that might have fallen there.
And while I was looking a voice came at me from behind,
"You really must be some One who is void of any mind."
Well, of course I turned around and looked around in front of me—
Till I spied a solitary Bank note sitting regally
High atop the other chair opposite my own.
The note—it was a ten—continued in a haughty tone,
"Any One who would think to find me in such a lowly place
Must have nothing in the way of brains in behind Its face."
"Well—" I said. "Enough!" cut in the note immediately.
"It's clear that you know nothing of my noble history.
Therefore you must sit and listen, and utter not a word,
As I tell you everything you should already have heard."
I then did as I was ordered and sank into my easy chair
To listen as the note revealed its history to the air.
"I'll begin at the beginning, just before my birth,
When One exchanged whatever It could spare, of any sort of worth,

For whatever goods or services It desired to obtain—
When anything was used in the trade of lack for gain.
Though barter did enable One to make more of what It had,
It was an inefficient way to turn a minus to an add.
Too often One had something another wanted to acquire,
While the other had not anything One wished to have or hire.
Now, as life is much too short and much too long on need
For One to waste It trading without the greatest ease and speed,
Something had to happen to set every trader free
From the wastefulness of barter. So I began to be.
I say "began to be," for I did not happen overnight.
Instead I was a while in coming all the way to life.
What slowed me down somewhat on my way to being whole
Was the stuff that I was made of—it was nothing more than gold.
Oh, that is not to say that I had no appreciation
For the substance that played host to my worldly incarnation.
To my mind, in fact, gold had just the qualities
To materialize a thing so material as me.
Gold was malleable and beautiful—and rare enough as well
That alone and on its own it could cast a worthy spell.
Another fitting trait was its divisibility.
Gold could be divided up into different quantities
Without losing its identity, without ceasing to be gold.
Golden bits and pieces were nothing less than smaller wholes.
Unlike things like cows and shirts and functioning machines—
Things that ceased to be, when broken up, what they had fully
been—
Gold, however broken up, was ever truthful to its name.
A bar of gold was no more "gold" than a tiny golden grain.
And since golden bits and pieces could be easily rejoined
Into larger wholes of every size and quantity of coins,
There was no price too large or small for gold to justly pay
In the easiest and most exact of compensative ways.
And lastly, but not leastly, was its lasting quality,
Its immunity to time and change—its immortality.
Gold did not decay or fall apart or cease to be itself,
While most every other thing in time turned into something else.
Thus gold could utterly be trusted to store One's worth away

For an hour or a decade or forever and a day.
Golden actuality—an eternal, ageless being—
What more could I have asked for to substantiate my meaning?
A whole lot more in fact, a whole lot more than gold,
For gold, alas, was something One could easily forego.
As One could neither eat it nor wear it to keep warm,
Its absence caused but little stir and was never really mourned.
The problem that I faced, then, when I first began to be,
Was the limited demand for the substantial part of me.
Though people thought it useful and handsome to behold,
They did not believe their lives relied on their possessing gold—
Which they simply had to do if I was to ever wholly be,
If there was ever to be such a thing as real and true money.
That purely worldly part of me had to come to be
Everything to every One to fully realize me.
But for gold to be believed to really be money,
It first had to play my role for every One to see.
It had to act convincingly in front of every One
Like that very special something it was destined to become—
The one and only means by which all could be obtained,
The universal go-between in the business of exchange,
The one thing each and every One would willingly accept
In return for goods or services It had for sale or let.
But gold, such as it was, could not act at all like money
Without some acting help from my human understudies,
From those Ones who understood enough my all-important role
To act sufficiently convincingly for quantities of gold.
It was up to Ones themselves, then, to make every One believe
That gold had worth beyond the worth One actually perceived.
But then it would be Ones who would be subsequently blessed
When gold achieved its greatest worth and I my whole-liness.
Therefore Onekind owed it to me, and to its selves as well,
To persuade its every One, by the suasive means of show and tell,
That gold had a character that was extremely honourable,
A quality that made it so completely valuable
That any One with enough of it could purchase anything
And any One with all of it could buy up everything.
Of course so many proved so suasive in their individual roles—

In the way they spread the word and accumulated gold—
That more and more all the time perceived ever more behave
As if gold was the only means to anything One craved.
And the farther spread that view the deeper grew the conviction
That I was the truest of all things and no character of fiction,
Till gold at last became every bit as good as me
And I every bit as real as real could ever be.
From then on all of value was in one way wholly equal.
In one way it was all made of the same material.
And since every form of wealth was made of purest gold,
One traded in the same thing, whate'er It bought or sold.
So One had not to work so hard to find a trading partner,
As It had had to do so much back in times of barter.
Any One would trade with It if It had enough of me,
Just as It would trade with any One who had enough money.
Thus did I reduce One's costs in time and energy
And enable It to fill Its voids much more easily.
And since One could go through needs and wants faster than
before,
One could well afford to need and want at least a whole lot more.
So that's how I empowered One to make more of Its life,
How I enabled It to profit more and pay a lower price—
How I brought It that much closer to the most and least extremes,
Where One could make the most of life and reality of dreams.
And in light of all the room I made for more to be more pleased,
It's no wonder Onekind found me so very easy to believe
And no wonder I went on from then to grow in my extent
And lose matter all the faster all the further that I went.
Yes, those early golden years I spent in the coinage state
Were not just years of growth for me, but also years of losing
weight.
Indeed, no sooner had I gained my full materiality
Than things began to happen that would disembody me.
Those possessed of hoards of gold sought a place to store their
coins,
Where their hoards of me would not be lost, nor would they be
purloined.
And they found a helpful goldsmith, who—though not a place—

Had just the place for storing gold, called suitably a safe.
And having found just such a place, they left without their hoards
And with nothing more than paper notes to show for all they'd
stored.
Of course, all they had to do to turn their notes back into gold
Was turn them back into the goldsmith for the money they had
stowed.
Until then, however, their precious savings would be safe
From the needs and wants of other Ones to fill up inner space.
In fact, the goldsmith proved to be so good at guarding hoards of
gold
That It never lacked for buyers of the service that It sold.
Ones came and went with money in a never-ending flow
That filled Its safe perpetually with half a safe of gold.
And the longer that Its safe remained half full up of me,
The more the goldsmith thought about the inefficiency
Of leaving so much gold to sit and fill up space inside a safe,
When it could be filling up no end of needful, want-full space.
But it wasn't till It thought of all the money It could pocket,
By helping more to help themselves to lives of higher profit,
That the goldsmith started loaning out the idle part of me
And thereby introduced the bank into actuality.
And as the money was repaid on time, as the bank got clean away
With loaning other people's gold and making idle money pay—
As It wasn't caught at all short of the money that It owed
By too many Ones at once trading in their notes for gold—
It continued to sell loans to those of insufficient means
To procure themselves new lives that were closer to extremes.
And since more Ones had more means to spend or to invest
On or in creating all the more from all the more of less,
There was an increase in the use of Ones and worldly nothings
In creating yet more somethings, or greatly valued things.
Nothings, by the way, were the raw and natural things
That composed the natural world and meant not anything.
That is, they had not any value, no power at all to please,
Till they were transformed into somethings that sated wants and
needs.
Thus, by loaning money out it had promised to protect,

The bank was doing more than making money off of debt.
It was loaning money out that wasn't working but at rest,
And thereby giving more the means to spend or to invest
On or in creating added wealth for Ones to buy,
So they could earn the more and share the more in the wealth supply.
The bank was helping make the world a fuller, richer place
For more than just the Ones with hoards of gold inside its safe.
And what with all the added wealth there was then evident,
More Ones were spending more and more gold was being spent
And less was being saved and stashed inside the banker's safe.
So the bank had less to offer in the way of saving grace
To those who wished to borrow to invest in making more—
In adding yet more wealth to the swollen, worldly store.
No One was to worry, though, for the bank had hatched a plan
That would provide it with sufficient gold to meet the loan demand.
What the bank exactly did was make bank deposits pay
Instead of charging for the service of stashing gold away.
It gave those with gold to save more reason to deposit
By paying for the right to use their money to make profits,
Instead of charging them for saving their precious hoards of me,
While loaning out their stores of gold to others for money.
It also promised to return the owners' stores of gold
Any time they wanted back all the money they had stowed.
And since gold gathered gold dust in interesting amounts
When it was left for any time sitting in a bank account,
Any One with any gold to store for any time
Was driven to deposit it where it would grow in kind.
Thus did the bank acquire yet more gold to loan about
And a debt for all the interest it had promised to pay out.
It then simply raised the price on the golden loans it sold
To raise the money it had promised to pay for hoards of gold.
And as the banks— That's right, the banks, for there were getting to be more—
So well did it pay to lend out others' golden stores.
And as the banks never failed to pay the owners back their gold

When they traded in their bank notes for the money they had
stowed,
Bank notes came to be regarded as synonymous with gold
And accordingly quite capable of playing money's role.
Those with paper bank notes, then, could settle their accounts
By passing on their bank notes without reclaiming their amounts.
Indeed, as bank notes were so light and had next to naught at all
To speak of in the way of depth—they were two-dimensional—
One could carry round upon Itself a pocketful of dreams
Without drawing any notice, without straining pocket seams,
Especially as all bank notes were of the same paper size,
Regardless of the quantity of gold they symbolized.
And One could get multiple receipts in exchange for Its hoard,
Each one equal to some fraction of Its total golden store,
So that One could spread Its gold over time and over space,
Instead of spending all at once in some one and only place.
No wonder then that notes were passed increasingly around
While their quantities of gold filled the safes and weighed them
down.
But only till the gold was lent to those who needed funds
To achieve still more of more for themselves and other Ones.
And since little paper bank notes were playing money's role,
Some borrowers repaid their loans with notes instead of gold.
And when the bankers saw the trust their paper notes had gained—
When they saw their notes and gold were regarded as the same—
They could not help but think of a most freehearted scheme,
A scheme that promised to make real and true the wildest of all
dreams:
The Dream of making everything from nothing more than naught,
Of creating gold from something which caused no One any thought
And loaning it to every One with the drive but not the means
To help realize for every One the greatest of extremes.
Only if more money could be easily come by,
If there easily was enough of it to fully satisfy
The continuous demand for loans of money to invest
In creating ever more out of ever more of less,
And enough for growing incomes to buy the ever more—
Only if there could be, quite easily, more money than before—

Would the journey to the greatest good be free of growing pains
And take the minimum of time to yield the maximum of gain.
Only if I grew as easily as did One's wants and needs
Would each One lead the fullest life that It could ever lead.
But gold was much too hard to find and too much work to mine
For its quantity, with easy speed, to ever-upward climb.
However, if the banks employed their most freehearted scheme—
The one that promised to make real and true the wildest of all dreams—
More money could be readily and quickly realized,
So all could make the very most of their precious, little lives.
And so the banks took advantage of the faith their notes had earned,
Not to mention all the ins and outs of banking they had learned,
And started loaning out more gold than e'er they had within their safes,
By loaning paper notes out in its nonexistent place.
They began creating everything from naught but paper notes
And selling loans of it to those who would make of it the most.
And those notes went on to make the world an ever-richer place,
Ever fuller of the sort of things that filled up inner space.
Of course they only managed that because the notes were thought to be
The equivalent of hidden gold and thus as good as me.
As for me and what I thought, well, I wasn't really sure
Of what to think of me, or of even where I were,
For then I seemed to me to be in more than just one place
In a body that exhibited more than just one face.
Indeed, not since my golden egg days, not since my incubation,
Had I felt such a muddled, such a dubious sensation.
Was I there or wasn't I, wherever paper notes were placed,
Or did I still in fact only have a golden face?
And as I watched all the banks welcome sums of gold inside
And loan out paper notes as though the gold had multiplied,
I wondered what would happen if all, who could, did demand
Their paper turned to gold before their eyes and in their hands,
For the notes that passed from hand to hand as things were bought and sold

Were really nothing more than bankers' promises of gold.
And there was nowhere near the gold in all the bankers' safes
As there were paper bank notes circulating in its place.
Though they trusted not completely the paper notes they used,
Ones did believe enough in them to leave me quite confused
About my real identity—or my real identities.
Was I gold or gold and paper in my materiality?
I simply would not know till I was fully one or both,
And such I would not be till the truth was known about the notes.
In time, of course, the notes were shown to not be all they seemed.
But then all were so much closer to the most and least extremes
That none could see a reason to feel deluded or deceived
By what the banks had gone and done with what they had believed.
In fact, what the banks had done had proved to everybody
That worthless paper notes could just as easily be money,
So long as each and every One believed in perfect unison
That they were absolutely everything to each and every One,
And so long as there was something there to protect their
    preciousness—
To see there never was so much of them that they were valued less,
And there never was so little that all could not do all they could
To do the greatest number the greatest quantity of good.
So no One really cared when it was finally revealed
That the gold behind a note wasn't necessarily real—
Especially when the government assumed control of money,
Of the size of its supply and its worth to everybody.
As the government was less concerned with its own private gain
Than with the benefit of every One who dwelt in its domain,
It was considered the least likely to abuse One's faith and hope
And the power to make money out of naught but paper notes.
Indeed, once the government had introduced The Bank to oversee
The practices of private banks and the creation of money,
None could see a reason to distrust the paper form
In which I was officially and utterly reborn.
Nor could I see any reason to feel I had been cheapened.
Rather I saw only proof that faith in me had deepened,
So much that my reality no longer so relied
On the value of the substance I went around inside.

And then there was the fact that in my latest elements
I could easily and endlessly grow greater in extent,
Till I was everywhere in everything and between everybody—
Something I could not have done as only golden money.
So there I was and here I am, more real than e'er before,
Weighing less than ever and yet weighing even more.
What I mean by that is I've lost matter from my being,
And yet I matter more—I have grown in worth and meaning.
And I have grown in my extent, in the size of my supply,
Till there are none I'm not between and naught I do not occupy.
But that isn't any wonder in light of what my growth has done
To make the world the place it is for each and every One.
Nor must it come as a surprise or any kind of wonder
That I've been losing paper weight to become no more than
numbers,
In order to keep pace with the rate of transformation
Of worldly, natural naught into the goods of satiation.
What with the growing size and speed of the average appetite,
It's imperative that I achieve the travelling speed of light.
If I'm to do that, though, to attain the maximum extreme,
I must move from place to place without passing in between—
Without passing through in body, for matter is opposed
By something called inertia when it stops and when it goes.
It must overcome resistance to change its place or state.
It must expend more time and energy to accelerate.
The less matter is involved, then, the less inertia interferes
And the easier and speedier things travel far and near.
Thus I must be completely matter-less to be completely free
To go as fast as light, which is as fast as fast can be.
Consumption is consuming, then, the material of money,
So fast that very soon there will be nothing left of me.
But even if I vanish, even if I disappear,
I will e'er exist, I will always be most here,
Because I am the medium of easy, fast exchange
Between the realms of reality and the dreamier domains.
I make One's dreams materialize right before Its eyes
And enable It to live the most ethereal of lives.
Indeed, as more and more have realized that ever more and more,

I have grown more real with time than I ever was before.
And soon I'll be so real that I'll be there for all to see,
Even though there will be nothing more than numbers left of me.
And though you might well think it nothing that numbers can be
seen,
They can only be perceived at all because of what they mean.
For numbers have no substance, though they number things that
do.
Two is just a concept that is symbolized by 2.
And as numbers have no matter, they can move extremely fast
Through the air and down the wires and through tiny pipes of glass
On nothing more than coded bursts of high-speed energy.
So, as numbers, I can get around almost instantly.
And since numbers are more endless than paper in supply—
In truth, they are so infinite no number is too high—
I, as numbers, can grow endlessly and never near an end,
Unlike all the other, lesser things on which a life depends.
And now I've reached the state in my materiality
Where there's nothing more material than immaterial me,
You simply cannot doubt that I am absolutely true,
Lest you not have the biggest cake and eat the whole thing too,
Lest too much of your natural naught remain as only waste,
And no One ever realize the greatest inner space.
On the other hand, if you believe utterly in me
And never show the slightest doubt in my reality,
I'll make your world an ideal place, despite the natural waste,
A terrestrial heaven full of goods and endless, inner space.
I can do such things, and with the absolute of ease,
For I am now more real than real could ever be."
And you know, no sooner had that note finished saying "be"
Than the hare appeared from nowhere and dived madly for the tea.
Then a battle did break out between the wilful two,
A war of which the likes you see right now in front of you.
And I too watched that battle, just as you are watching yours.
But I also watched the note as it looked down upon the war.
And once the situation had grown adequately tense—
Enough so the Bank note was consumed by the suspense—
I grabbed the note and left without leaving by the door,

A war of which the likes you see right now in front of you.

Just the way my guests had done when they had left some time before.
After listening to a ten so full up of itself,
While feeling rather empty, I simply could not help
But trade the haughty thing for something with more stuffing
Than only just a tenth of both everything and Nothing.
SNAP!

[*The hare sails backwards to disappear into the wall of blackness at the edge of the floor as the tea lashes past One to disappear, along with the teapot, into the blackness at the opposite end of the floor.*]

O: [*Rises from hunkered position between table and toppled box seat. Retrieves box, sits down and looks around for the hare.*]

ZF: The hare has knocked Itself out again, apparently—and the tea. But then It will persist in doing such a hare-brained thing as trying to have tea at a tea party that's all for Nothing.

O: What's so hare-brained about trying to have tea at such a party?

ZF: No One's supposed to drink anything at a party that's wholly for Nothing. After all, the whole party's for Nothing—for drinking Nothing, eating Nothing. Indeed, no One but Nothing is even supposed to be at a party entirely for Nothing.

O: Then who's the party for?

ZF: For Nothing, of course—or any space that's there in place of any One who isn't at the party.

O: In a sense, then, a party that's wholly for Nothing is a party for every One and no One—or a party for all the spaces in all the places of all the Ones who aren't at the party.

ZF: That's right. It's the one party where every One is equal, where no One can be any more the life of the party than any One else.

O: So you three have not only bent, or broken rather, the rules concerning Nothing-type parties by showing up at this one, you've invited another One to join you besides. And, from the looks of all the waste about the place, you've consumed a lot as well.

ZF: Ah, yes, but what's a party without even the appearance that a good time is being had at it?

O: I don't know. A party that's not a party? So all the empty containers strewn about us are only for show. It's all a masquerade, in other words. It's all Nothing masquerading as a masquerade party—or masquerading as a certain very famous tea party where nothing made sense as well. Or it would be, if it weren't for you three and me.

ZF: What three are those exactly?

O: Who exactly are you? How should I know? I can't see your real faces.

ZF: [*Smiles knowingly and nods.*]

O: Oh, I get it. That's how you go to a party for Nothing without showing up at it. You wear costumes so it looks like you aren't there—the One you really are, that is. You look like some One or something else, so no One can see you're there. You disguise your presence with your apparent absence and thereby manage to both be and not be there. And by dressing up as a purely fictional character, a being that does not really exist, you manage, in a sense, to keep the space you occupy empty.

ZF: [*Continues to smile knowingly.*]

O: But I've blown your clever little ruse. I'm here at your party—physically as myself. Because of me, your party hasn't turned out to be the party you planned it to be.

ZF: Ah, but this party's not over yet.

O: I'm not sure I like the sound of that, especially after seeing the tea go for me the way it did. It put me in a dangerous position. If I hadn't hunkered down below the table when I did, who knows what would have happened to me? So I can't help but wonder, a little at least, if your little party might be out to put an end to me. Then I'd really know Nothing, wouldn't I?

ZF: Oh, but that's no way to get to know Nothing. Tales are a much better way, don't you think? Or did you not enjoy my tale? Did it not tell you how Nothing is the reason there is more and more good things in the world all the time?

O: It did more to tell me how money has become nothing.

ZF: Oh, but you forgot the capital "N." Can't forget that. There's a world of difference between nothing and Nothing.

O: Yes. I wanted to ask you about that.

ZF: You can't, though, because there's only time enough left for me to tell you my next tale—a tale with no end.

O: A tale with no end? I haven't got forever, you know.

ZF: Which is why I'm going to tell you only the tail end of it.

O: But you just said it has no end.

ZF: What I meant, but didn't say, was it has two ends that fit end to end, so the thing never ends without beginning all over again. And now that I think of it, it wasn't the tail end so much as the front end of the thing that talked to me. So I'll tell you what that end said instead.

O: What are you talking about?

ZF: You'll see.

While walking down the street one day I met a marvellous
machine.
It was running round in circles—It went where It had been.
I said, "Hello," and It looked up and grinned from gear to gear.
"What makes you so very happy?" I posed to toothy ears.
"Why, money makes me happy! In fact it's everything to me!
I can never have so much that I'm as pleased as I can be!"
"Oh, please don't turn away again. I'm not sure I heard you right.
Did you say money does and doesn't fill you with delight?"
"I don't know that I did, although I do suppose it does.
I do suppose, as well, I always end up where I was."
"Of course you do," I said, "going round and round that way.
Why ever do you do that? However can it pay?"
"There is nothing that I do that I do not do for more
Than ever that I give to gain the thing I do it for.
And that thing of course is money, the answer to my dream
Of a life more rich with meaning than the life of a machine.
As One yourself, you too must dream of the power to be free
To do more than you are driven to by pure necessity.
Alas, but in reality power has a price
That necessity dictates One must pay for with Its life—
Unless One find a way around the cost of being free,
Such as I have found in money. *Free money*, actually.
With enough such money One can get such things for naught
As It needs to really do the things It freely dreams It ought

And spend the life It would have spent working for such means
On doing as It chooses to and realizing dreams."
"But I do not understand," I said, "for money isn't free.
One can't acquire it for nothing, at least not legally."
"Oh, but on the contrary, it can rightly be obtained
By getting more for less than One need give up in exchange.
So long as both the parties gainfully concerned
Believe they are receiving quite sufficient in return,
A profitable exchange can easily be made,
Despite any inequality that might be hidden in the trade.
Which is really quite a good thing,
Considering the following:
As no One can do any more than One alone can do,
One cannot outdo Itself without help to do it through.
But if One must do for others for the things they do for It,
Despite Its many added powers, One can realize no profit.
Still, One who has free money in sufficient quantity
Can pay others for their powers without paying personally.
Indeed, One, who has amassed so great a quantity
That it makes itself as fast as One can spend it endlessly,
Need only show Itself to attract the love and the respect
That are others' to bestow on those they deem of good effect.
Wherever that One goes the servants follow It in droves
And goods gravitate toward It like they've nowhere else to go.
Alas,
But it takes a lot of free money to live a priceless life.
Still, One can quickly gain a lot by simply doing right.
One must see to it that nothing goes for nothing in Its life,
Save to One before it goes to others at a price.
One must buy up all It can as if it were but naught
And sell its every bit as if it were the utter lot,
And never give enough away for any One to see
That while It is getting less One is getting money free.
And, with every bit of free money One thereby does obtain,
One must invest in adding more to Its freely gotten gains—
At least until such time as It has gained the liberty
To simply watch as Its free money shows It magically

That One's greatness is not measured by how much One has
done,
But by how much One can do while It is doing for no One."
"Though your ears may not be geared to hear what I'm about to
say,
I am compelled to say it and thus will say it anyway.
Though as toothy as your ears is your ever present grin,
You look as though the life you wear has worn extremely thin.
If you have spent no more on obtaining more for naught
Than the difference you made from a little for a lot,
Then you should be as good as new, as good as when you started.
Instead you look as good at heart as you sound good-hearted.
If you have always spent enough of that which you have made
To reimburse yourself for what you yourself have paid,
And have only risked what you have gained in freely gotten funds
On such means as you have found to simply multiply their sums,
Then however have you come to waste so very much away,
As though all that you have raised yourself is less than equal
pay?"
"It seems I'm not the only One who seeks to realize
A greater reason for Its being than because It is alive.
Indeed, more and more all the time are striving to attain
Lives of greater meaning through freely gotten gain.
More money, then, is being made than is being earned
And prices rise as though untied from the world of their concern.
And the freer money grows of the stuff of worldly more,
The more money is the only thing that One is living for."
"But that makes no sense," I said, "for money's not the why.
It's just a part of the how to the life you visualize."
"Not any more it isn't, not for me at least,
Now I've found, through money, a life of utter ease and peace.
Once it simply simplified the problems of exchange.
Now it utterly demystifies the question of my Aim.
For every One to realize a life worth living for,
Every One must get for less what must be got for more.
Every One must do, then, what every One cannot—
Talk about an Aim that is truly all for naught.
Nor is that the only proof that all is all for naught.

Just look at One's capacities for knowledge, doubt and thought.
Paradoxically enough, the more One grows to know,
The more It knows It doesn't know of all there is to know.
And since the more One knows of all, the more It knows but
naught,
The One who knows but nothing knows the whole, entire lot.
And the One who knows completely all doubts absolutely not.
And the One who has no doubts has no need at all for thought.
And since doubt and thought only cause displeasure and unease,
But for whose existence One would be at peace and pleased,
Mine is a knowing smile, or the smile of One who knows
The utter easiness and peace known by only those
Who know absolutely everything for what it really means
With that certainty of knowing known only by machines,
Which never have the slightest doubt, lacking as they do,
The power to know anything, let alone if it is true.
The only way It all makes sense is if It's all for naught,
And if One gives not anything but nothing any thought.
And nothing is more Nothing than the freest of money—
Than that which is not based upon materiality,
But purely on the faith in money's power to supply
Something out of nothing any One has realized.
Only if Its mind is free of uncertainty and questions
And of the power of necessity to force on It directions,
Can One grow to know Its own mind to any great extent
And freely follow where It leads with Its very own intent.
And as nothing is less vital to the furtherance of life
Than money that deigns not at all to pay a worldly price,
I can think of nothing better to occupy my mind
And force out every care, save the One it leaves behind,
Than that nothing that is everything for which it is exchanged
And nothing that is anything that can actually be gained.
Thus it is that I am free of every dictate from without
To tail myself exclusively round and round about."
"But surely you are mad to hold such an empty view.
It is obvious that trusting thus takes a lot out of you.
Already you are in a most emaciated state.
Indeed, you circumscribe a zero as you circumambulate.

And soon you'll be a zero that has swallowed itself whole,
Like the snake that ate its tail and left no snake to play its role."
"Ah, but I will be perpetually happy and at peace,
Because, starting where I end, I can never really cease."
Well,
As I did not have it in me to watch so much devotion
Drive Itself around the bend with perpetual emotion,
I made to take my leave and be gone as I had been
Since before I ever met with any marvellous machine.
Besides, I was already late for another get-together,
Still, it was a party all for Naught and Nothing lasts forever.
And so our meeting ended, just before it ever start,
With me remaining there to wave and watch as I depart.

O: You really are quite mad, aren't you?

ZF: Isn't every One?

O: Every One here is—and Two, Three and Four. First it was names and numbers. Now it's a Bank note with a life of its own and a machine that chases Its tail for worthless money. What next?

ZF: [*Slides Its box seat down to sit directly across from One.*] How about this? [*Rummages in Its pockets, pulls out a folded piece of paper, unfolds paper. From the spreading folds falls a second smaller piece of paper, which stands on two of its corners and timidly peers at One from beneath the fully open sheet. The larger sheet appears to be a blueprint—or blackprint rather—for a Money Machine.*]

O: Where did you get that? Draw it yourself?

ZF: Drew it from my pocket just now. You saw me. The ten too, apparently.

O: I thought you spent that.

ZF: Oh, I did. But they do come and go, you know—tens, I mean.

O: Not so full of itself, I see. It must be some other ten than the one in your first tale.

ZF: No, it's just paper is all.

O: Instead of gold?

ZF: Instead of nothing, actually. It shouldn't be there at all now—not bodily—to work fast enough for One. Nor in such a

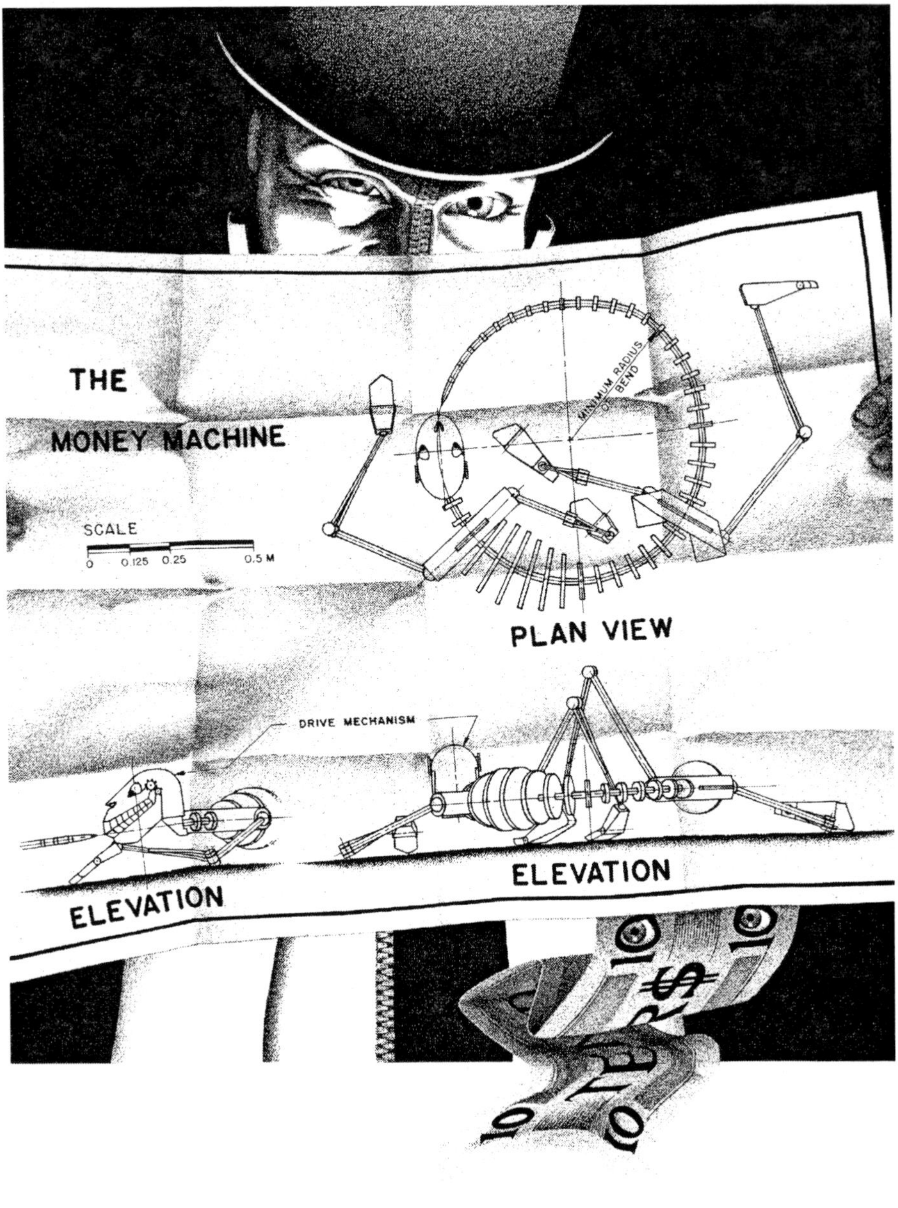

The larger sheet appears to be a blueprint—or blackprint rather—for a Money Machine.

small number. Still, it is money—it is Nothing—and therefore counts for something, unlike so many other things today. [*Refolds paper and puts both paper and note back in pocket.*] Well, time's up. Gotta go. My absence is owed at another party. [*Pushes seat away from table and stands up.*]

O: I take it it's another party for Nothing. [*Backs seat away from table and stands also.*]

ZF: The only sort we ever attend. And if I know the hare, It's already there taking on the tea. That leaves just the mouse and I to tidy up then. [*Walks over to mouse followed by One. Prods mouse with foot.*] Okay, you. Time to pick yourself up.

O: [*Solicitously to Zipper Face while mouse endeavours to wake up and get up.*] Do you think maybe I could tag along? I know I don't have a costume on, but couldn't I just say I was some One else, some One who doesn't even exist? I wouldn't impose on you if I didn't feel such a need for company. I don't want to be left alone again. Not here. Being alone here makes me feel like nothing at all.

ZF: Like you're here but you're Naught, sort of thing?

O: Yes.

ZF: [*Smiles, doffs hat with one hand and with the other grasps the zipper's exposed tab. Mouse more or less follows suit.*] Ah, there you see, the party has turned out to be all for Nothing after all. [*Both whip their zippers down to reveal nothing inside and are gone.*]

O: [*Gapes at the crumpled costume heaps lying amidst the rest of the party debris. Suddenly hears a brief series of muffled thuds emanate from beyond the wall of doors. Whirls and dashes for the doors. Bursts through one of the doors to catch sight of something shrinking into the depthless, white distance. Races after the thing and gains some on it before it suddenly collapses into a stationary heap. Quickly closes on the heap.*]

Both whip their zippers down to reveal nothing inside and are gone.

Four

One: [*Standing over a panting, twisted heap of diamond-covered arms and legs.*] E-Excuse me, but are you all right?

[*The heap unravels and rights Itself somewhat to reveal a wide-eyed fool—or at least a wide-eyed One dressed up as such.*]

Fool: Wh-what happened?

One: You tripped and fell, I think.

F: Oh. Well, gotta run, gotta run! [*Struggles to get up.*]

O: Wait, wait! Don't run off yet! You'll only fall again if you do. Obviously you're too tired to pick your feet up, and you have to pick your feet way up in those runners. No, stop for a bit. Catch your breath, rest your eyes. To be honest with you, your eyes are rather hard on my eyes. Don't you ever blink?

F: Don't have time.

O: Well, I think you should take time. And I think you should get yourself some different shoes. You may be trying to run like a fool, but you'll be a crippled fool if you continue running in the shoes you've got on.

Wh-what happened?

F: D-did you just call me a fool?

O: Well, you're dressed like a fool, aren't you?

F: I-I am? [*Looks Itself over in disbelief. Hears a ringing in Its ears and reaches up to investigate.*] H-how?

O: I take it you had no idea you were dressed like that. [*Sits down on the ground across from the fool.*]

F: [*Looking not so much lost in thought as lost as to how to begin to think.*] Wh-when?

O: It's no good asking me anything. I don't know anything anymore.

F: Surely The Dream can't have had anything to do with it.

O: The dream? What dream?

F: [*Suddenly focuses on One.*] *The Dream*: the one I've been running in.

O: You've been running in your sleep then.

F: I've not been running in my sleep; I've been running in The Dream.

O: But you haven't just been dreaming you've been running. You've actually been running.

F: Because The Dream I've been running in is real. At least it has been becoming more and more so for quite some time now. It first started coming true when we discovered stones, bones and tree branches, and it has been coming truer ever since.

O: I beg your pardon. Stones, bones and tree branches?

F: Our first tools.

O: Tools?

F: Yes, you know, those things One uses to change nothings into somethings.

O: I know what you mean by tools. But stones, bones and tree branches? What sort of things could you change with them?

F: Us, for starters.

O: But you can't have been nothings, surely.

F: Oh, but we were. All any One of us had were a clawless set of hands and feet and a blunt collection of teeth. And none of us had any strength compared to some of the other animals we competed with for existence in the world. Nor was any One particularly fleet on Its feet.

O: My, but you were a primitive bunch, weren't you?

Wh-when?

F: A bunch of helpless fools, yes.

O: You dressed like fools then?

F: No, I mean we were a bunch of know-nothings. None of us had a clue what was going on around us. And because none of us knew anything about anything, not One of us could do anything about anything. All we could do was keep our eyes peeled and hope we saw what was happening soon enough to be able to get away fast enough, or to get to it fast enough—if it was something good instead of bad—to get a share of it before the stronger, more intimidating animals drove us away from it.

O: But being ignorant is not the same as being foolish. Not if One can't help being ignorant.

F: Oh, we couldn't help being ignorant all right. We couldn't help doing anything we did then. In fact, it wasn't until one of us inadvertently got the idea to join with a stone, a bone or a tree branch—I forget which exactly—that any one of us had any real power to amount to any more than nothing. A "One" with a capital "O," instead of "one" with a lower case zero at the head of it. Not much of a One, mind you, but more than any one of us had added up to before. And of course, when the rest of us saw what One could do with a stone, bone or branch batting for It, we too began making somethings out of ourselves with stones, bones and branches. After that we could not only better defend ourselves and put up more of a fight for a share of what little there was of any good to us in the world, we could also grind grains, crack nuts and dig roots and tubers out of the ground. In other words, we could make food of things that had been nothings to us before because we had been unable to get at them. Even better, though, we could make better tools than the ones we found lying about in the world. For example, we could use one stone to chip away at another stone to create a sharp, wedge-shaped stone, which we could use to easily cut, split, chop or scrape things. We could also affix a wooden or bone handle to the sharpened stone to make it even easier to use.

O: A stone axe sort of thing.

F: Or knife. Just two of the many new and improved tools we were eventually able to make yet more of ourselves with. Albeit not easily. In fact, the more power we had to make a difference in the world around us, the more work we had to do, because our tools had no power of their own—except for the horses and oxen we used to carry loads or pull wagons and ploughs for us, and they weren't real tools. How could they be, what with being living things and all? Trying to get other living things to work for One is like trying to play croquet with flamingos and hedgehogs as mallets and balls, if you know what I mean.

O: They're given to wandering off?

F: To not following orders. Apparently, other living things have their own reasons for being that have very little, if anything, to do with us. And they're such needy things on top of that. Not only did we have to make horses and oxen act like tools for us, we had to take care of them too—feed, water and shelter them and all that. A real tool, though—that's another thing altogether. The only reason it exists is because One or more of us created it, and the only reason any One created it was to work for One. As well, a real tool has no need whatsoever to be paid for its work. It has no need at all for any more than it absolutely must have to do the job it was created to do. (Not even a real tool can make something out of real nothing or utterly empty space.) A real tool is utterly indifferent to itself, just as it is to everything else. It cannot care at all about anything. It simply is, and for no more reason than to empower One or more Ones to make more of the world than they can without it. A real tool knows of no reason whatsoever for being, yet it will always give all it has to give and never demand any more in return than it absolutely must have to give its all. It is utterly incapable of doing otherwise.

Or so we know now. We didn't know that then of course. The only real tools we had back then had no power of their own to act for us. They relied entirely on us for whatever power they had to fulfil their reasons for being. No One could ever actually get any more work out of any such tool than It put into using it, despite any appearances to the contrary. Oh, One could deliver a far more effective blow with a sharp, iron axe than It could with Its own soft, bare hand, but the tool's power was still One's power. One only had to cease working with the tool and put it down to see how much the tool could do without One's help. The axe could only lie there doing nothing. In using an axe to chop wood, One simply transmitted Its own power into a thing more suited to the task than the edge of Its own hand: the sharp, iron-hard edge of the axe. And of course the axe had to exist before One could chop wood with it. Therefore, we not only had the work of using our tools to create somethings out of worldly nothings to do, but also the work of creating the tools that would empower us to create such things. And it wasn't as though any One of us had any power to spare, what with how little power One had to change the world on Its own and how short was the time It had to be in the world. No wonder every One dreamed of acquiring the free power to make more of Its life.

O: Is that dream anything like the one you mentioned earlier?

F: The very same. *The Dream* with a capital "T" and a capital "D." The one dream we all shared in common—and all had trouble realizing.

How could any One make the most of Its life who had to spend almost all of It extracting from the world those somethings It needed to do with Its life as It dreamed? And there was so much more in the way of goods One could have, since we'd discovered how to cause still greater quantities of valuable plants and animals to grow around us. After we began raising only the most hardy and productive of useful plants and animals, we were able to produce so much food for ourselves that we no longer had to all be farmers to feed us all. Instead some of us could be spinners, weavers or tailors, leather-, wood-, metal- or stone-workers, painters or potters or whatever. Each One of us could even specialize in a particular type of work. And that meant we could all have a lot more than enough to eat all the time. Even so, what good to One were goods It had too little time and energy to put to use in making good of Its life? They were a lot less good than they could have been, that's what—because our real tools were of so little help to us. All except for free money, that is.

O: Oh no, not you too. I just came from a party where very little else was talked about.

F: Doesn't surprise me a bit. Powerful stuff, free money.

O: Hardly. It's worthless stuff.

F: Not if it's real free money. Not if it's free money that has been made by selling others more for less.

O: I beg your pardon. One who sells more for less can only get less for more in return. It can't get more for less in return. It can't get anything back free.

F: Not without somehow reducing the cost of supplying the somethings One sells. Not without finding a way to produce more from less. The best way to do that was by reducing the amount of One-type power that went into realizing anything of value, as it was the most persistently expensive thing that went into making somethings because It refused to be taken for granted. Rather It was forever trying to get more in return than It gave of Itself. But then One had to use up power to do anything at all in life and It had so little power to go around.

Alas, but all our real tools were so helpless without our help back then that the only way we had of reducing the part any One played in the production of a supply of somethings was by reducing One's part without reducing Its part.

O: An impossible feat, by the sound of it.

F: Only by the sound of it, though. To know how we did it, you'll have to listen to a lot of technical stuff about supply and demand and such. I know how the technicalities of life bore One. It's why we've always put all we could of them off onto our tools.

O: I can take it. Especially as there's nothing else to occupy my mind right now.

F: I'll make it as simple as I can, if that's any consolation. Now let's see. How shall I put it? Well, just for example, say One performed ten different operations with ten different tools in producing each of Its somethings. What One could do to reduce the work that went into creating each something was hire ten other Ones and assign each One the task of continuously operating one particular tool. Even if none of the Ones One hired had any training in the operation of the tool It was to use, each One would take only one-tenth the time to learn Its part in the production process—one-tenth the time, that is, that One Itself had taken to acquire the knowledge and skills It needed to alone produce Its supply of good things to sell. Better still, once trained, all ten of One's workers would be able to perform all ten operations at once without stopping, or with each stopping only long enough to pass Its completed bit of work on to the next One in the production line, and to receive from the One before It in line the next bit of work It had to do—unlike One who had to cease performing one operation to perform the next operation in the process. Thus could One produce an almost continuous flow of finished somethings, instead of the much-interrupted flow that One produced working on Its own. Have I lost you yet?

O: No. You're saying that One could produce ten times as many somethings in no more time than One took to alone produce one-tenth as many.

F: Right. And because each worker would have only one-tenth of the skill that One had, each could justifiably demand to be paid no more than one-tenth as much as One could demand. One would have to pay Its ten low-skilled workers for producing ten times as much as one highly skilled worker only as much as It would have had to pay One highly skilled worker. And because One could pay so little for so much, One could easily sell each something in Its much-enlarged supply of somethings for appreciably less than before. And One who sold Its somethings for a lower price than any One else around who sold the same things naturally attracted all the buyers there were around for such things. Better yet, if One was the first One to thus produce so much more from so much less, It could charge the highest possible lower price for Its goods—till either every One who could and would pay so much had bought all It needed or One of One's competitors discovered how One had produced so much more from so much less and began to do the same, if not because of what It could personally gain from doing so, then because of what It would personally lose from not doing so, as soon as possible: all of Its customers and all the money It could have made. As more and more such somethings became available for the lower price through other suppliers, One would find it increasingly difficult to sell any such things It had left—unless It dropped Its price still lower, which One could well afford to do, having up till then charged so much more than It had actually spent to produce so much. And round and round and down and down the price would go, as supplier after supplier endeavoured to make the most money It could and to defend Itself against the actions of Its competitors—until the price was no higher than was necessary to make producing only as many such things as there was desire enough about with money enough to pay just enough to make the undertaking a worthwhile one. In other words, a reasonably profitable undertaking, even if not an extremely profitable one.

Of course, One's competitors would not be One's only imitators. Any One with an eye to getting as much as possible for as little as possible—in other words, every One—who saw what One was doing and saw It could do the same with Its own business, would just naturally do so, consequently inciting any rivals It might have to find out what It was doing and do the same, thereby making the new way of working to create worldly wealth the only way of working to create worldly wealth and lowering prices all round to where they could be paid by the much lower-paid workers that would then be all over the place.

O: So that's how you reduced a worker's work without reducing Its work. You reduced the worth of Its work without reducing the amount of time and energy It had to spend working. You simply reduced the knowledge and skill each worker required and thereby the amount of money It could demand to be paid for Its services. You simply devalued a worker's work.

F: In Its own mind as well as every One else's. Just prior to the introduction of increased specialization, a worker, using the tools of Its specialty and Its own special knowledge and skill, had worked alone or with very little help to create a supply of a particular kind of something for Itself and other Ones as well. A worker had had a special power that few, if any others, had and no One could easily and quickly acquire; a special power to mean more to others and Itself as well; a special power to make a significant, singular difference in the lives of others as well as in Its own life. Now however, any One, in relatively little time, could learn to do what It did—and in a little more time, do it without thinking. In other words, every worker could expect to be easily and quickly replaced if ever It left Its job or disappeared for some reason. No worker was likely to leave a noticeable hole in Its absence, certainly not a hole that would take any real time to fill again—with what would soon be a void of a different sort. Work had become so mind-numbingly simple and repetitive that it was harder on a worker than any work had been before. It took so much out of a worker, even while demanding so little of It, that it left It feeling like nothing more than a lifeless tool. Indeed, it was almost as though a worker's reason for being had become the same as that of a simple tool, that being to perform the same simple operation over and over again throughout its existence for other than itself.

O: I don't see how any One could have got any One else to do such demeaning work for It in the first place. Surely no One would have chosen to do such work.

F: Not knowingly anyway. That's why employers looked for the willingness to work thus among the young and yet untrained—till falling prices forced even highly skilled workers to accept such demeaning work. And because any new worker acquired so little skill and so little money through Its highly specialized employment, It could not choose to leave and go into business for Itself—certainly not with much chance of doing so. Even if It had worked as a highly skilled worker before It had been driven out of business and into doing highly specialized work for another, It could not go back to working as It had before, not only because It could not make enough money to set Itself up in business again, but also because It could not supply enough cheap enough on Its own to compete with Its more specialized competitors.

O: So all that stuff you said about real free money being money that was made by selling others more for less wasn't true. Not *exactly,* certainly. Not every One actually ended up getting more for less—or even as much as It had before for the time and energy It spent working. Some actually ended up with what amounted to less for more.

F: Most did actually. Only a relative few really ended up with more for less, and they ended up with a lot more for a lot less. But then that was the best we could do at the time with nothing but a lot of helpless tools to help us out. We could realize only enough free power to supply relatively few of us with any amount of it. And because we'd done what we'd done, we could then realize more free power for ourselves. By making less of ourselves as workers—or at least of those of us who actually did the work of changing worldly nothings into worldly somethings—we were then able to make more of our real tools. By acting more like real tools, we were then able to empower our real tools to act more like us—in our capacity as workers, of course.

O: How—?

F: By further dividing up the work of realizing somethings out of worldly nothings, we had made the work of the individual worker so simple and repetitive that the worker could be replaced by the simplest of power tools—which was the most powerful tool any One of us could have invented at the time. Though our knowledge of the workings of the world was growing faster than ever by then, we had not yet gained enough worldly knowledge and experience in tool creation to create the sort of sophisticated, multi-talented tools that would be capable of replacing highly skilled workers. The best any of us could do with what we had learned so far was invent a most simple power tool. Simple with regard to its powers, that is. A lot more complicated with regards to its parts. By means of a system that employed such things as levers, pulleys, gears and crankshafts, a new tool was able to translate the motion of a rotating wind- or water-wheel into the particular motion it needed to do its job—an up-and-down or back-and-forth motion or just the right speed of circular motion. Still, it wasn't till we discovered a way to put the powerful heat of fire to work producing electricity that we were able to transport free power through wires and cables to all manner of power tools wherever, whenever and in whatever quantities they needed in what seemed like no time at all. That's when we really began to free our tools to more fully fulfil their respective reasons for being. A tool could then work all day and all night, day after day and night after night, without ever getting bored, tired or sick—without ever feeling a thing. And that's not all; it could work harder and faster too. It could go through its simple motions at a constant, rapid speed. And it could generate a force far greater than any force any One could empower a similar worker-powered tool to generate. In fact, the strength, stamina and speed of our new tools were such that it only took one simple power tool to push successfully for the speediest possible creation and employment of more and more power tools.

See, whenever a particular type of simple power tool was invented and introduced into a particular step in a particular production process, the speed of the process increased so much at that particular step that the steps before and after it could not keep step with it. In fact, only the slowness of the worker-powered tool ahead of the new power tool stopped the worker-powered tool after the new tool from being buried in an avalanche of work. The new power tool could pass its work onto the tool after it in the production process no faster than the worker-powered tool ahead of it could pass work onto it. So instead of doing as much work as it possibly could, the new power tool spent most of its time waiting for the worker-powered tool ahead of it to give it something more to work on. Even if all the tools in the process, except one, were replaced by their equivalents in simple power tools, the one worker-powered tool left would hold up all the other tools. So, unless all the tools in a production process were simple power tools, there was little to be gained from employing any such tool in the process.

And another thing: the complexity of the new tools made them considerably more expensive than the older, more worker-dependent tools. They were more work to invent and build. So unless the new tools were able to work as much and as fast as they possibly could, they could not pay for themselves very fast. And they couldn't work as much and as fast as they possibly could, unless all the other tools they worked with were equally as powerful as they were. Which all added up to a lot more expense.

Not too much more, though, for by increasing work specialization we had also managed to create considerable concentrations of free monetary power. The thing about free power, especially such a universal form of free power as free money, is One can never have enough or too much of it, simply because it is power that personally costs One nothing to acquire. It is only ever cost that puts One off anything. Lower the cost of something, best of all, make it entirely free, and there's nothing to stop One from having to have that thing. Another thing about free monetary power: to use it is to lose it—albeit in exchange for the thing One uses it to gain. Unless that thing is at least as much free money as before, One ends up with less free power than it had before—less of that which it can never have enough or too much of. If, however, that thing is more free money than before, well, One ends up with more, instead of the same or less. And increased work specialization had left some Ones with considerable amounts of free money to invest in making more free money and other Ones with shining examples of the potential that existed for making free money by supplying others with more for less. In fact, any One with any money to spare—any money It could put off using long enough—could then put that money to work earning It more money without Its help—earning It free money, in other words—by purchasing a share of the cost and thereby the profits from the purchase of any new power tools by the bigger businesses. And of course, what with all the money there was about just waiting to buy new power tools to replace the old worker-powered tools, there was plenty of incentive for those with the capacity to invent and build such tools to do just that—as much and as fast as possible, so as to get in there first with the right tools and sell the most tools for the most money. The net effect of this feverish race to get there first and make the most free money possible was that every possible type of power tool was invented, built and put to work as much as fast as possible. And sure enough, the new tools, despite their being more complex and thereby more expensive than their predecessors, far more than paid for themselves by empowering their quick-acting employers to produce so much more from so much less that the latter were able to acquire goodly portions of money supplies elsewhere as well as even larger portions of the local money supply by supplying more Ones, both near and far, with more somethings for closer to nothing—or more simply, by providing more with more for less.

Even more, by empowering our tools, we had empowered ourselves to make use of still more of the natural nothings about us. We had empowered ourselves to create an even greater variety of tools and goods, as well as to improve the tools and goods we already had. And to know that we could make a great deal more of the world and thereby our lives was to know that we simply *had* to do just that. After all, no One had any time and energy to waste on living less of a life than It could possibly live. And none knew that better than those of us who had risen above the fog of cost that obscured the average One's view of life, the view of One who had to work for everything It got. Free of the long hours of hard, low-paying work that clouded the mind so the eyes could hardly see, the chosen few could—

O: Chosen few?! Surely you didn't call them that. Makes it sound like they had some sort of right to have so much while others had so little. And they only had so much because they had taken so much from others to get it.

F: And they had been able to take so much, because the rest of us had given it to them willingly. Each of them had offered us more for less, and we had accepted—no, leapt at—each One's offer. Not One of us had turned them down. They, above all, had given us just what we wanted.

O: They hadn't given it to you. They'd charged you for it—as much as they possibly could.

F: And we had paid their prices—of our own free will. Us and our inherent need to get more for less whenever we could. Never has it been just the relative few of us that has made us pay for their increased freedom. Always it has been all of us who have chosen them to be the recipients of whatever free power we could muster up amongst ourselves at any given time.

It has always been us ourselves we've had to save ourselves from. So long as we ourselves continued to play material roles in the creation of satisfying somethings from natural, worldly nothings, somethings would continue to be as costly as we ourselves could make them. And so long as we had to give so much of ourselves to gain the goods we needed to do as we dreamed with our lives, we would be left with too little freedom with which to make something of our lives. Any One, who did not pay with free money for something, only ever really paid with Its own precious time and energy—with life It could have spent more profitably, if only It had had the necessary free power to spend It thus.

But if any more than a small number of us were going to be free enough to fulfil our own reasons for being, we were going to have to free our real tools enough of their dependency on us for their power to fulfil their respective reasons for being. And to do that, most of us were going to have to expend all the time and energy we possibly could working and buying all we possibly

It has always been us ourselves we've had to save ourselves from.

could, so as to generate the maximal profits that would continue to incite all those, with the free means to do so, to invest all they possibly could in the creation, construction and employment of more and more tools with more and more power to provide more and more of us with more and more for less and less. Or at least that's how the chosen few of us saw it. But then, they could see so much better than the rest of us, occupying, as they did, positions of free power in the world that afforded them a clear and easy view of the potential for greatness that still remained in the world. In fact, they could see only too well compared to how most of us saw things.

O: I'll just bet they could.

F: Though the new power tools had relieved workers of the work of powering their tools, their work was still as simple and repetitive as ever, if not more so. And the pace of their work was more driving than it had ever been before, because the new tools now ran them more than they ran their tools. They had to run the harder to keep up with their hard-driving, noisy and dangerous partners. As such, not even keeping workers supplied with the education they would need to run and maintain increasingly sophisticated tools and ensuring them job safety, health care and income sufficient to get by on was going to be able to incite them to work any more than they absolutely had to in their view. If workers were going to be able to see their way to actually doing as the select few of us saw they simply had to do—if The Dream was going to come true as fast and fully as possible—some means of empowering them to see right through the costs of doing as they had to was going to have to be devised. Fortunately, a tool was not long in coming into being that would give every single One of us the vision It needed to see right through the costs of any- and every-thing to all that lay beyond—a tool we appropriately called television.

O: Television?

F: Never heard of it?

O: Of course I've heard of it.

F: But have you seen it? One has to see television to believe it.

O: I don't believe much of what I see on television.

F: You believe more than you believe you do. That's the great thing about TV: it teaches One without One knowing It's being taught. It does so by making information so easy to take in. To absorb information from Television, One doesn't have to know how to read. It barely has to know any speech. All it has to be able to do is see and hear with Its eyes and ears, talents most every One just naturally has. One then learns quite naturally from TV. And anything One does quite naturally It does quite easily, even without thinking.

Best of all, though, TV makes the dissemination of information easy. By means of the medium of television One can send the exact same message to huge numbers of Ones in little more than an instant. One can do the same with radio too, but radio's just sound, no pictures. And if a picture's worth a thousand words, TV's a thousand times better at spreading information than radio. Still, radio's better than books, magazines and newspapers. The problem with books, magazines and newspapers is they are so much more substantial than radio waves encoded with sounds—and images, in the case of television—that they are a whole lot harder to spread around. They have to be physically carried from wherever they're made to wherever they're to be sold. On the other hand, encoded radio waves—which are just about as immaterial as anything can get and still be there—only have to be transmitted into the air to spread themselves to radios and TV's everywhere, with a little help from satellites and such.

It's no wonder, then, that radio, and television in particular, soon became the preferred means of both spreading and acquiring information about the world. In fact, most every One who saw and heard TV, particularly color TV, came to regard the predictable, plodding black, white, black, white, black, white that was so characteristic of written works as just too dull to contemplate for even an instant. Even those works that featured pictures only featured stills, and stills tended not to hold One's attention near as well as the moving pictures of Television did. That's not to say that such means were not also put to work helping every One to see properly, only that TV, being the most efficient such means, was naturally the preferred means. Indeed, every tool for communicating information was put to work tunnelling through the haze of cost that obscured the view of most to provide every One with a clear, telescopic vision of the undeniable profit that awaited It. As every One knew, without thinking, that any gain It could get for free was unquestionably a gain, getting every One, including every worker, to believe deeply enough to see right through the cost of everything to all It needed to see—to all It needed to need—

O: What's that? Needed to need? Isn't that one too many needs?

F: Goodness, no. Every One *had* to need, *needed* to need, all the good things we and our tools could possibly produce. If It didn't, we wouldn't continue to realize our shared dream of free power as it ought—as it *had*—to be realized. As much as fast as possible, that is. For every One, who had to, to keep working and spending as much as fast as possible, every One had to keep needing as much as fast as possible. Not wanting. Needing. Because wants weren't pressing enough. They hadn't the urgency of needs. The satisfaction of a want can be postponed indefinitely, if need be. But not the satisfaction of a need, not without having a serious effect on One's well-being. And unless a worker did what It had to do to live the best, most meaningful life It possibly could, unless It worked as much as possible to buy as much as fast as possible, It would have a serious effect on Its being. It would end up wasting Its existence on knowing a less valuable, less meaningful life than It could have known.

That such might not happen, that no One might waste any more life than necessary, every One of us needed to need a growing number and variety of things—many of which many of us had never even dreamed of wanting—as much and as fast possible.

O: But if One hadn't even dreamed of such things, how could It possibly want them, let alone need them?

F: No One should ever have to do without just because It lacks or has too limited an imagination to see how well off It could be. Or do you believe otherwise?

O: No—

F: Well, there you are. And besides, most Ones have only to see such somethings as they have never even dreamed of, especially in the right light, to know only too well that they simply cannot afford not to obtain such things for themselves. Of course, by the right light, I mean that light which sets the gains from something so aglow that the costs of it cannot be seen for its blinding beneficence. Television is particularly suited to showing things in such light. Things on television literally glow with the appearance of substance. That, added to the fact that TV's have screens and screens are good for hiding things, or as filters, has made television an invaluable tool in the creation of our needed need. By hiding or filtering out all the hard-to-swallow, burdensome bits about something and allowing only its most dreamy aspects to pass through the screen into the eyes and ears of whomever is waiting on the other side, televised information can be rendered even easier to absorb—utterly easy, in fact. Of course, there has to be some One on the other side of the screen to take the information in or there's no point in broadcasting it.

Assurance of an audience was to prove no problem, though, as television, soon after its arrival in the world, was put to work providing every One with the dreamiest and most dazzling array of entertainment possible. In fact, the world of TV quickly became the world of our shared dream. In other words, a world where no One ever seemed to work who did not have an exciting job and was not attended by all the latest goods; a world where anything was possible, where any One could do anything and without paying in any real way to or for doing it; where every problem was solved and solved in what amounted to almost no time at all. Through the dreamy medium of television any One could experience all manner of exciting things, have all manner of exciting adventures, and all just like that. Nothing to It. Any One could see life as It was dreamed of, instead of as One was forced by the reality of necessity to see It—cost free and full to the brim of enriching possibilities. Best of all, though, television was so easy to take in and televised lives so easy to take part in, so undemanding of time and energy, that even those Ones who arrived home utterly exhausted from a long day of life-draining work could find within themselves enough remaining vitality to live It up somewhat through their TV's.

So, ensuring the presence of mind en masse at the debut of a new good—ensuring a large and attentive audience, that is—was simply a matter of presenting that good during the broadcast of one of the dreamiest shows on television. And the considerable moneys paid by the advertisers of new products to the producers of televised entertainment for time spots on such shows naturally made sure there was an ample supply of highly enticing, highly captivating shows to advertise on. Of course advertisers took care to present their goods in only the most gratifying and compelling light: in images, sounds and words that glorified the gains from such things and hid all their costs—except for any devastating losses One stood to suffer from not acquiring any particular good. Only the important stuff could get through, the stuff of substance. As for the rest—out of sight, out of mind, as One knows. Or rather, as One doesn't know—or shouldn't. After all, what One doesn't know can't hurt It—not in any way One is aware of at least.

Once every worker was empowered to see right through the costs of the wonderful somethings that awaited It to working with all Its worth to obtain those things, every single One of us was able to wholly play Its part in changing the real world into the world of our Dream with all the seeming naturalness of One who was entirely free to do whatever It pleased. From then on it seemed The Dream came more and more true all by itself—without any One having to give any real thought or effort to making it come true, just as anything did that was simply meant to be. And the world flowed with more and more goods all the time. Over rollers and conveyor belts, railroads and paved roads, airways and shipping lanes, flowed endless, growing streams of increasingly affordable goods to every One everywhere. Identical goods too, for the consistent accuracy and high speed with which our newer tools worked made it possible for every One to receive as good a good as any One else, the very same good in fact. All thanks to the Dreamy enlightening light of television—and radio and all the other tools of mass communication, to say nothing of the examples of consumption every One did Its best to set for every One else.

In fact, it even got so that no worker could bear to be out of work for any real time at all, lest It find Itself unable to furnish Itself with all the latest necessities of a meaningful life—which, in actuality, It could not do, even if It worked non-stop. See, as far as TV was concerned, every One was equal, regardless of Its capacity to learn or the quantity It earned. Television showed and told every One the same thing—which meant that it had the effect of utterly equalizing need. Through television every One came to share the exact same set of needs—every One came to need everything. Of course, every One could not have everything. For most of us, in fact, the equality of need went only as far as TV. It did not extend to reality. In the world of TV every One was free to need the exact same kinds and quantities of things, but in the real world every One was not equally free to satisfy Its needs. Not every One had access to endless, great sums of money—no matter how much It worked. Instead most every One could work as much as It possibly could and still only be able to buy but a small fraction of all It needed to be fully satisfied for any real time at all. Needing was one thing, filling that need was quite another. Even though more and more things were dropping in price all the time, with the creation and employment of increasingly powerful tools, there were always more and more things that most every One simply had to have—right away—and couldn't afford.

For many a One there was just no other way to escape the intolerable emptiness of unsatisfied need than by demanding to be paid more for working no more than before. (One had only so much time and energy to spend working.) But One alone had no power to press Its demand. One with a lot of other working Ones, however, could have an effect on things that could not be ignored. Inevitably, then, workers took to banding together to enforce their demands for higher wages. Of course the workers' demands for higher wages only raised prices and thereby reduced the value of the money they made. Everything just ended up costing more money. Sales and profits fell, dragging down with them the incentive to invest in the increasingly powerful tools that would increasingly realize The Dream for every One. But only till a tool came along with the power to get to the very root of our problem with One another—the brains behind It. Then came the brain-power tool.

O: Brain-power tool? A tool that could think, you mean?

F: Let's just say it could do things One's brain could do. Calculations, for instance. In fact, it could do all sorts of things

One's brain could do, because it could add, subtract, multiply, divide and compare quantities.

O: But that's only five things and they're all mathematical. Not what I'd call all sorts.

F: All the same, the brain-power tool could do all sorts of brain work because it could perform those five mathematical operations—and because some of us had since discovered that those five mathematical operations could be used to convert a great many kinds of information and related instructions for working with those various informations into forms a tool could take in and work with. Thus a tool that had originally been created to make very fast and precise work of time-consuming and tedious calculations was empowered to do a lot more than just mathematical chores—especially when advances in micro-electronic know-how rendered it possible to make a brain-power tool small enough and cheap enough to be installed in just about any other kind of tool. Indeed, brain-power tools became so compatible with their more physically talented counterparts that the next thing we knew more and more of our tools were able to think for themselves, so to speak, and all manner of work was disappearing or becoming even more specialized. That included office jobs too. Being more concerned with collecting, processing, storing and transmitting information than with collecting and transforming worldly materials into various kinds of somethings and transporting them to distribution centers about the world—being work of a more mental than physical nature—office work had remained, till then, largely unaffected by advances in the independence of our tools. After the introduction of the brain-power tool, though, not only more and more of those tools whose purpose it was to handle the material things of the world began to work still more and more on their own, but also tools whose purpose it was to handle the immaterial things of the world—the quantities of information that empowered us to keep track of the material things of the world, ourselves included. As with our more physical tools, our information tools began by assuming the most simple and highly repetitive mental tasks and advanced from there to increasingly complex tasks.

As for us, it was all we could do just to keep up with them all. For all their awesome powers, our tools were still quite dependent on us. Though a good many of them were extremely fast and thorough learners, not one of them was brainy enough to learn entirely on its own. Nor could any one of them manipulate the variety of things with the same ease and dexterity that One of us could with Its own flesh and blood hands. Nor could any get about as easily as One of us could. Till our tools could make sense of the world on their own and handle things and step and climb about at least as good as any One of us, they would still need us to work with and look after them.

That's not to say, of course, they weren't of considerable help to us in freeing them once and for all to free us once and for all to live the most powerful, most valuable lives. On the contrary, our latest tools were quite sophisticated and adept enough to be of vast help in the design and construction of still freer tools. Every newer and more powerful tool empowered us to realize a yet newer and more powerful tool in still less time than before. As our tools evolved faster and faster, their "life" spans grew shorter and shorter, as did the lifespan of many a worker's job.

Indeed, speed, which had always been important, became extremely material and in its wake immateriality. The more material or massive something is the more time and energy it takes to move about. The same applied to any business. So, when speed became extremely material in the significant sense, a business had to become as immaterial as possible in the physical sense to remain at all material in the significant sense. It had to become as small as possible, so as to be able to change course or location as quickly and easily as possible. If it was not possible for a business to be small, then it had to be composed of a network of loosely joined and easily disposed of parts. It could never be any bigger than it absolutely had to be at any time to make the maximum possible profit. Once any business had profited all it could from any of its component parts, those parts had to be quickly disposed of and any new ones that might be required bought or hired as soon as possible—and for only as long as association with them resulted in sufficient profit. As workers were more difficult to dispose of, owing to their demands for consideration, tools were naturally the parts of choice wherever possible, especially since they worked a lot more constantly, consistently and speedily than workers did. As well, obsolete tools were quite literally dead weight and thus could be got rid of with the greatest ease and speed. A tool may have been more material in the significant sense to begin with, owing to its considerable cost, but it was rendered immaterial and disposed of much more easily than any One was, and would not—could not—demand all the costly coddling One inevitably did—holidays, sick leave, coffee breaks, safe working conditions, and so on.

No wonder, then, work was faster and faster growing harder and harder to find all the time—especially work that lasted any real time at all and paid well enough to furnish One with anywhere near enough power to acquire all the latest necessities of life. Tools had acquired so many of the powers to be found within Onekind, and in so much greater measure, that only a very few things remained that any One could do to really help out a tool. Or to put it another way: the skill required of any one worker was pretty much the same skill required of any other worker. Which meant not only that there were a lot of workers about who could do any one job, but also that jobs had grown so rare and precious that no worker would risk Its job for the sake of the demands of any other worker. There was no longer any strength in numbers to be found between workers, weakness more like. Those who were hard-working and lucky enough to have real work—as opposed to those who supplied the few remaining simple-minded skills to still deficient tools—worked like mad to keep their jobs. When they weren't working their long days and long weeks alongside their awesomely powerful partners, such workers were busy retraining themselves to meet the demands of their next, newer and yet more powerful partners. Instead of spending their free time on discovering the range of potentials they had within themselves, they spent it studying information on the potentials inherent in their tools for meaningfully being. Tool manuals became the most read of books, in other words.

O: [*Shakes head.*] What I don't understand is why you didn't just share the work that remained amongst yourselves and give every One more time and energy for a personal life.

F: Aside from the fact that it had become the most natural thing in the world for One to spend all the time and energy It could working and buying all It simply had to have, work was just about all there was left to *do* with One's life. In the desperate search for work, more and more workers had looked to the private sphere for employment—for work doing things for other Ones, Ones had traditionally done for themselves or had traditionally done for each other for free, or at least not for money. Thus had every possible relationship One could have with Itself or any One else been eventually transformed into a means of making money. And of course, wherever any of us ran to make money, our real tools soon followed—if only to save us from our propensity to cost each other as much as we could—till there was a super-powered tool to do any- and every-thing any One could possibly do in life. And when all was said and done by other things for One, what life was all about was having those things. The only problem was that to have those things, One had to have the money to pay for them, and to acquire the money It needed, One had to have work.

[*Suddenly falls silent and gives One a look like nothing would have, if it had a face to look at One with.*]

O: Well? Then what happened?

F: Th-then I tripped and fell and you asked me if I was all right.

O: And the next thing you knew you were here?

F: [*Gapes blankly at One.*]

O: You don't by any chance know where here is, do you? It's nowhere, as near and far as I can see. In fact, far looks as near here as near does far. Didn't you find running here to be an awful lot like running on the spot? Ah, but you were too busy running in that Dream of yours to see how you were dressed, let alone where you were or where you were going.

F: [*Says nothing while Its eyes wander off for an aimless look at the scenery.*]

O: What are you going to do now? There can't be any more point in you running in The Dream. Nor—I hope you'll forgive me for saying this—any more point in your being at all, except to be the helpless fool you've so obviously made of yourself. There's nothing left for you to do with your life—nothing that can't be

Th-then I tripped and fell and you asked me if I was all right.

done a whole lot better and faster by some tool. That getup of yours is all that remains to you. You came all that way all that fast just to end up where you started. Well, not exactly. Whereas you weren't a helpless fool to begin with, you are now. You even look the part. You really should have known better, you know. You had the capacity to. Only you went to sleep on the job and let that Dream of yours do all your thinking for you. And now the joke's on you, apparently. You even have to laugh at yourself, if only because it's painted on.

F: As I've come this far, I may as well go all the way.

O: All the way? What do you mean "all the way"?

F: All the way to where I was before I was even there at all.

O: What? Before you even so much as existed?

F: I may as well end it all, once and for all. I only wish that ending it all wasn't so hard for One.

O: Oh, but there's probably a tool now with the power to empower you to freely and easily end it all.

F: You're probably right.

O: I'm sorry. I didn't mean to sound so heartless. What I should have said was: be careful what you wish for; you might get it—especially with all the free power you've thoughtlessly realized for yourself.

F: [*Eyes grow wide again and begin darting madly about.*] What's that noise?!

O: What noise? I don't hear any noise.

F: [*Looking back in the direction It came from.*] Did you see that?!

O: See what?

[*Suddenly, on the very edge of One's hearing is a hum, barely audible for the lowness of its pitch, and at the very edge of One's vision the horizon line is showing barely perceptible signs of movement. As the hum rises ever faster in pitch, the white falls as fast before the onrushing black. Both Ones barely have time to stand, turn and look at each other before the blackdrop hits them with an inaudible force that sends One tumbling end over end.*]

[*One sits up to find Fool and everything else—such as it was—gone, or at least lost to view. Blackness is everywhere. One cautiously crawls about, groping with hands and probing with voice for a touch or a sound of the other One. "Gone, near as I can tell. For good? I wonder. No point in wondering too much. Not when I've got so much wondering about myself to do. What am I supposed to do now? I can't even walk about in this. Before I could see for untold miles, even though there was nothing to see. Now I can't see any distance at all. Do I even dare stand up? Might as well. The ground doesn't seem to have changed—except for its not being white, or light, anymore. It seems to be as utterly hard, level and empty as ever. Makes me think I could walk along it—so long as I was careful." One stands, sways slightly, and takes a few tentative steps forward—and continues walking forward, till . . .*]

Five

One: Ouch! What the— ?

Two: I must say, when we meet, we really meet.

O: Is that you, Two?! It sounds like you!

T: At least I sound to you like the Two of me.

O: You don't sound to me like there are two of you. You sound to me like the one named Two. I thought I'd seen the last of you when the three of you dropped out of sight.

T: Three? There has only ever been the Two of me.

O: I was referring to Three and Four as well as you. Why aren't they with you now?

T: How do you know they aren't? You can't even see me.

O: But I can hear you. And from what I hear, you're speaking for yourself now and not the three of you—for Three and Four too. You're saying "I" instead of "we" and "me" instead of "us." Where are Three and Four anyway?

T: They stayed behind this time.

O: They stayed behind you last time.

T: But not near so far behind as they stayed behind this time.

O: I don't blame them. You never let them say anything. Not that Four looked as though it cared much, but Three looked as though it might have liked to participate more. As for me, I can't even enter your presence without you knocking me about somehow. That was some rap on the head you just gave me.

T: I didn't rap you on the head. I was just standing here when you walked up and knocked your head against mine.

O: Yeh, I'll just bet you were. In fact, now that I think about it, there was something odd about the way we bumped heads.

T: What was so odd about it?

O: We bumped only heads. We didn't bump anything else. I had both hands stretched out in front of me, groping where I was going, and yet I didn't feel you there at all—till my head hit your head. I don't see how I could have missed you till then.

T: Nor do I. It's time we had some light to see by. [*Suddenly there is light.*] Hey! Hi there!

O: You're upside down!

T: I beg your pardon. You're the One who's upside down.

O: Don't be absurd! You'll fall on your head!

T: No, I don't believe so. I believe you might, though.

O: Oh, stop fooling around, Two, and come down here right now. I can't talk to you when you're upside down like that.

T: Why not? Do my words sound inverted to you?

O: Of course not.

T: I don't sound upside down to you then. So why can't you talk to me as I am?

O: Because you don't look right to me. In fact, it's a wonder I can see you at all. Where did the light come from? Where *is* it coming from?

T: Where does it appear to be coming from?

O: From somewhere below the top of your head, but I can't see where.

T: Then don't bother. You can see by the light even if you can't see where it's coming from, and that's all that matters.

O: No, it's not.

T: Why not?

Hey! Hi there!

O: Because it doesn't make sense, that's why. The light's not coming from anything.

T: What makes you think that things have to come from things?

O: The world I come from. It can't be just any sort of things either. Certain things have to come from certain other things.

T: And that makes sense to you?

O: Of course it does. How else am I going to know what causes what? Where I come from I have to know such about things, as things do not just happen there just because I wished them to. I have to make them happen. Or some One does. Especially somethings. Where I come from somethings do not just naturally present themselves to One in whatever kinds and quantities One desires wherever and whenever One desires them. Certainly not as a rule. As a rule, somethings have to be made to be real, and no One can realize a particular something without knowing the sorts of things such a thing comes from and how those things go together to make that thing.

T: *That* doesn't make sense to you, does it?

O: What? That One has to know things to realize the things It needs in life? I don't know why it shouldn't.

T: Well, it's not as though you're really any good at getting to know things, is it? I mean One can only ever really be in one space at one time, and from where- and when-ever It is, One can see only so far and wide and deep into the world around It. It can't see things too big, too small or too near or too far for It to see, or things that happen too fast or too slow for It to see. Still less, One can see only so much at once of the limited amount It can see. It certainly can't see every little thing It can possibly lay eyes on. One's attention doesn't spread that thin without becoming barely attentive to anything. The more things One tries to take in at once, the less each thing stands out in Its mind, till everything becomes nothing more than a rather insignificant part of one great background. And the more mindful One is of any one thing, the more It loses sight of everything else around that thing. Isn't that so?

O: Well—

T: Of course it is. And that's only the half of It. There's the rest of It too—the world without and about One. That world is chock-full of all manner of things, things which themselves are full of all manner of smaller and smaller things. Even the spaces are full of molecular things that contain still smaller and smaller things, so that every worldly thing is surrounded on all sides by other worldly things, which in turn are surrounded by still other things and so on and so on all around the world. And what with there being no end of things, nothing happens between any two things without affecting the other things in the world around them, which in turn affect the things around them and so on and so on. Nor is anything that happens the result of just the things involved in it, for those particular things wouldn't have come together as they did to cause that particular thing to happen at the particular place and time it did, had not a lot of other things happened previously to put those things just there just then. Everything that happens or comes to be is the result of an intricate maze of other things and the cause of an intricate maze of still others. And things are happening everywhere all the time, both inside and outside of things. And there's little, simple-minded you in the midst of It all thinking you can make sense of things.

O: Simple-minded?!

T: Perhaps I should have said narrow-minded instead. After all, it is the narrow scope of your perceptual powers that so confines and defines the limit of your power to know things—that and the shortness of your life. You've not got much in the way of time to get to know things either. And in light of the shortness of your narrow-minded life, perhaps "small-minded" is better yet than "narrow-minded," where you're concerned.

O: Is that so? Well, I've more of a mind than I need around here. Far more. Not only is there almost nothing at all to even so much as sense here, what I've seen and heard of the very little there is here has made no sense at all. Present company included. Just look at you, hanging upside down like it's normal or something.

T: I could say the same about you.

O: But I'm not hanging upside down.

T: Oh, but you are in my view.

O: That's not a viewpoint. That's just you hanging upside down.

T: I would expect you to have such a narrow outlook on things. Just as I would expect you to have no end of trouble making any sense of such a world as the one you hail from.

O: It's not as overwhelming as all that. For the most part, things don't change so much so fast there that One can't follow anything. Not naturally anyway. Not the things I can see at least. Nor is everything all that different from everything else. There's a lot of different things, yes, but there's a lot of things of the same kinds too. Things repeat themselves quite a bit. And like I said before, certain things always give rise to certain other things, more or less anyway. Enough so One can see enough of the same things happening as a result of the same and other things that One can learn enough about such things to be able to predict fairly accurately what will come of a meeting between them. Nor does One have to rely solely on Its own powers alone for Its knowledge of the possibilities inherent in the world around It. One can learn a lot more indirectly through other Ones than It could ever learn on Its own. And not just through those Ones nearest One in space and time. There are books, magazines and newspapers, and the telephone, radio and television, and the computer too, through which One can obtain all manner of information from all manner of Ones from all manner of past and present places. And thanks to others of my kind, there are even things like microscopes and telescopes that can empower One to see things too big, too small, or too near or too far for One to see of Its own power alone. Even things to show One things that happen too fast or slow for One to see at speeds One can see them happen at. From my single place in worldly time and space, then, I can see a whole lot farther, wider and deeper into worldly space *and* time than I could ever see by my own power alone.

T: But the perceptual powers of other Ones are not appreciably different from One's own. Even with any of the instruments you mentioned to help It see more than It can see with Its own eyes alone, One can still take in only so much at a time, whichever One It is. And in a world where everything is directly or indirectly connected to everything else—where nothing happens that is not the result of a whole lot of other things and the cause of a whole lot more—nothing is ever simple and straightforward enough for any

One to be able to grasp it in total—or to even come close to doing so.

And then there's the power of Ones to communicate with One another—if One can call it that. For One to be able to clearly understand another One, One has to be able to see things from the other's point of view. And One can never do that, and not only because no two Ones can ever occupy the exact same place in space at the exact same time and so see things from the exact same angle. Not even if things typically happened exactly the same way more than once—which they do not—and more than One could witness an event from the exact same place in space, not even then could two Ones witness that event from the exact same vantage point. No two Ones are endowed with the exact same set of physical traits—the exact same body—with which they do or experience the exact same things in the exact same order in the exact same ways at all the exact same times and places. No two Ones live the exact same life, in other words. No two Ones can. And because no two Ones can live the exact same life, no two can have the exact same view of life—of being in the world in the midst of everything. And just to compound the differences between Ones: for One, believing is seeing as much as seeing is believing. Whenever One looks at anything, It looks at that thing as much through what It has already come to believe about the world—as much through Its mind—as through Its eyes. In a sense, One sheds as much light on anything It sees as any outside light source does. But instead of simply revealing to One what It can actually see about a thing, the light of One's belief tends to blind One to certain visible features of a thing while highlighting certain others. It reveals most to One what One expects to see and least what One least expects to see, whether either is there to see or not. Whatever One has already discovered about the world affects whatever else One discovers about it. Of course, as no One lives the exact same life as any other One, no One's belief about the world is exactly the same as any One else's—at any point in time. No One sheds the exact same light on anything It sees as any other One seeing the same thing at the same time, but from a different angle of course. No two Ones perceive anything from the exact same point of view. And because a particular thing is never the exact same thing to any two Ones, the word for that thing never means the exact same thing to any two Ones. In other words, no two Ones speak the exact same language, even if they speak the same language. And of course, what goes for words goes for images too. The image of a thing no more means the exact same thing to any two Ones than the word for it does. No One, then, can accurately and completely understand another. No One can see clearly through another One. The most any One can do is only seem to see through any One else.

O: You sure are one for exaggerating, aren't you Two?

T: I'm not One, I'm Two.

O: Yes, you're *Too* alright, Too as in "too much." *You* certainly see things from your own extremely contrary point of view. The way you see it, One is so unlike every One else as to be the only One alive, the only One who ever lived. But if the differences between Ones were all that great, we would never have been able to communicate well enough to accomplish so much together as we have. That we have been able to join powers to furnish so many of us with enough nourishment, warmth, safety and a great deal more besides is proof we can understand each other.

T: On the contrary, it only proves One can use other Ones to get more out of the world than It ever could alone, without ever really knowing any One else. Or even One's own mind, for to turn to other Ones for help in getting to know and make more of the world is also to expose One's mind to the viewpoints of others—even if not to ever fully understand any One of them.

O: So? Where's the harm in that?

T: You don't see it? I should have thought it would be most obvious to you, with me standing right in front of you as I am.

O: You're not standing in front of me; you're hanging upside down in front of me.

T: In your view.

O: It's not just my view. It's the truth. I know because I can feel gravity pulling at my feet, at my whole body. So I know it's pulling at your head.

T: It is pulling at my head, just as it's pulling at the rest of my body—feet first.

O: It is not.

T: Ah, but that's just what you have to keep telling yourself to hang on to your own view of things, your own mind. You cannot admit of the validity of my worldview without admitting that you do not know even the little you believe you know. You cannot allow of my viewpoint without allowing your own doubt, your own vulnerability. It's no wonder you find my stance on things so upsetting.

O: That's not the reason. It's because I'm afraid you'll fall on your head. That and I find it disconcerting talking to an inverted face. It's not something I'm used to doing.

T: Are you absolutely certain there's not more to it than that?

O: Where you're concerned, yes. I know you're trying to confuse me, just as you tried to do the last time we met.

T: The first time we met, you mean?

O: The first and the last time we met, then. I don't trust you, Two. And because I don't, it's going to take a lot more than you hanging upside down like that to make me doubt my conviction regarding up and down.

T: It's really too bad, then, that I didn't insist that Three and Four accompany me. With them on my side I would have outnumbered you Nine to One, instead of just Two to One. Surely that much more in my favour would have made an impression on you.

O: Having witnessed your regard for Three and Four, I can't see why they would have sided with you—unless it has to do with the way you looked together. The three of you looked like you belong together, like you've got some sort of family resemblance thing going. At the very least you looked to be part of the same outfit, almost to the point of appearing to share the same skin. But as to whether or not you're all of the same mind, I don't know. Oh, I saw how Three and Four went along with you and your last little bit of nonsense—or how they *appeared* to go along with you. In other words, I'm not so sure they did. Three seemed incapable of standing up for itself and speaking its own mind. As for Four, well, Four was a hard figure to figure out. I couldn't tell whether it stood back and let you do all the talking because it was totally behind what you were saying or because it simply refused to participate in what it considered to be a meaningless exercise. All I can say with any certainty about Four was that it was there in body. Where it stood mentally, I've no idea. Only the Two of you made any real show of having a mind of your own, while both Three and Four made no real show at all of not having minds of your own as well. So even if Three and Four did both side with you in your attempt to turn my thinking around and me on my head in the process, I would have been no more inclined to give into your claim of being right way up than I was to give into your claim of being nine instead of three. You'll not drive me crazy by shear force of numbers. I'll see to that. I'll always insist on proof more substantial than Three and Four standing behind you, lending visible support to any of your mad claims before I'll even begin to consider believing you, Two. I'll even insist on more proof before I'll believe that you yourself in fact believe what you say and that you're not just making a show of believing it in order to confuse me. I know it's only too possible to know one thing and say another.

T: Oh, you do, do you? However did you come to know that? Could it have been through associating with others of your kind? It wouldn't surprise me a bit, you know. I know all about the propensity of Ones to intentionally deceive One another. If it is to another One's benefit that One receive inaccurate or deceptive information—as it is bound to all too often be in a world where there is only so much to go around—the other will likely see that One receives such information. In other words, another is naturally prone to show and\or tell One only what It wants One to know, or what is to Its advantage that One *believes* One knows, for One must not in fact know, lest One possess the potential for worldly power that real such knowledge would invest One with. The need of another to have power One does not have obviates the satisfaction of any need for such power that One might have, so far as the other is concerned. In a world where every One's power to ensure Itself a sufficient share of what life-sustaining and life-enhancing stuff there is to be had from that world depends on Its knowing more than others know, duplicity is bound to abound.

O: I'd expect you to know all about duplicity, Two. After all, duplicity is all you've ever been about. Even your name smacks of double-dealing. And you did claim to be Two in number. That's as good an admission of being Two-faced as any I've heard.

T: Ah, but you deceive yourself, I assure you.

O: No, I don't. It's you who deceives me—or is trying to—by telling me it's the gravity weighing you down that is keeping you up like there that. I may not know what's holding you up, Two, but I know it's not gravity. I can feel it holding me down, and it can't pull both ways. There would have to be two grounds—

T: For both of us to have sufficient grounds to behave as we're behaving? Well, obviously there are sufficient grounds, sufficient ups and downs, for us to do as we're doing.

O: There are not. There only appears to be, and only because the light we're seeing by only shows so much of us to each other. Now that I think about it, it strikes me as rather convenient that the light is only bright enough to illuminate the upper portions of our bodies. It cannot reveal the truth at the feet of either of us. Nor can I see where it's coming from, so I can't see what to move to move it to where it can show me what I want to see, namely whatever it is that you're hanging from. The purpose of that light is not so much to reveal, as it is to deceive.

T: Which makes it no different from any other light, where One is concerned. That's not to say, of course, that all light is out to un-enlighten or mislead One. Only that One cannot help but deceive Itself by trying to learn anything about the world without and about It, and It cannot help but deceive Itself all the more by depending on other Ones for a greater knowledge of the world. It's bad enough when One must perceive things at One remove from the world—through Itself, in other words. As It is, One can't really see for looking, not without missing untold more than It will ever see. But if One must perceive things at more than One remove from them, then One can only hope to possess a knowledge of such things that is as many times removed from real knowledge of them as the number of Ones It has to go through to receive information about them. Deception piled upon deception is the result of One depending on others for information about anything. Even if One could count on the honest, open help of others, those others would still only pass on to One what they believed they saw. They would still deceive One, even if unintentionally. Because, for every One, believing is seeing as much as seeing is believing, there will always be as many versions of any story as there are Ones who participated in or witnessed that story's unfolding. And none of those versions will be precisely the same as One's own version, had One Itself been there to perceive that story being realized firsthand.

Even if One could rely on the totally objective reporting of other things than Ones for its information about the world of Its being, One would still be able to take in only so much at a time. Nor does One have all the time in the world to get to know things. Far from it. So far, in fact, as to be almost no time at all in comparison to how long the world has existed and will continue to exist. Nor can One pay attention for even as long as a full lifetime. Most Ones must spend roughly a third of their lives in the unconsciousness of sleep. In other words, One simply has neither the capacity of mind nor the capacity to live long enough to even begin to make sense of things. Not in a world where everything is directly or indirectly connected to everything else—where nothing happens that is not the result of countless other things and the cause of still countless more. In such a world nothing is near simple enough for such as One to fully understand. Nor does anything begin that does not then begin to end. And in a world where nothing lasts, nothing can have any great significance. All must come and go as though the rest can get on just as well without it as with it. That goes as much for One as it does for anything else in that world.

In the face of all that darkness, how can One imagine Its view of the world to be anything other than a complete fabrication? How can One view any effort to make sense of anything as anything other than a complete waste of time?

O: Easy. One's life depends on One knowing whatever It can, regardless. Without some understanding of things, however scant and superficial, One can have no power or freedom to do with Its life as It desires—as It dreams. One cannot even be assured of Its own survival.

T: What you say may be true, but is it right?

O: Of course it's right. If what I said is true—which it is—then it's right. Or I'm right.

T: You might be right about your situation, but is your situation right about you?

O: What nonsense are you foisting on me now, Two?

T: Just this:

Should One's being be but nonsense?
Should One—who cannot know—

O: Hey, wait a minute. Sounds like another rhyme. The last time you recited a rhyme you just up and disappeared—or down and disappeared—the moment you finished it. You're not going to do that again, are you? You're not going to just up and desert me, are you?

T: Don't tell me you would miss me. Don't tell me you enjoy my company, after all.

O: It's preferable to scrabbling around alone in the dark. Even if the light didn't leave with you—which I have a feeling it would—without anything to shine on, I doubt it would do me much good. Not unless I wanted to look down on myself.

T: And no One wants to look down on Itself, does It? Up to, yes. Down to, no. No, I won't desert you directly on finishing. I will remain with you for time enough after. Now, where was I?

O: Very near the beginning, I should think.

T: I shall begin again then.

Should One's being be but nonsense?
Should One—who cannot know—
Be forced to spend existence
Endeavouring to know?
Or should One's life make sense to One?
Should that which One must do
To live a life of worthwhile sum
Be that which One can do?

Which "should" should be reality,
The true one or the right?
Or should One simply cease to be
To make sense of Its life?
If One's life was simply nonsense,
It would matter not a bit
If One continued in existence
Or simply up and quit.

But One's life is not so meaningless
As the truth would have It be,
Which is why there are both more and less
Of more than quantity,
And why there is a word like "should"
Within reality,
And why wrong and right and bad and good
Are possibilities.

So . . .
Comedy or Tragedy?
Plus or minus One?
Up or down, which should It be?
Max- or mini-mum?
As if One could choose not to lose
While the truth need of no more
Than its mere material proof
To be too real to be ignored.

O: I'm not even going to ask you where you got the ink blots from. Mostly likely they're from the same place the light's coming from. I do want to know what exactly it was you just said, though. That One's life is but a tragedy and a farce to boot, so long as the truth has anything to do with It?

T: So long as the truth is not the right truth, One's life is nonsense. So long as reality dictates that One must endeavour to make sense of things, even though It hasn't the power to really understand anything, One's life can make no sense. Least of all good sense.

O: But that's ridiculous.

T: Isn't that what I just said?

O: No, that's not what I mean. I mean what you said is ridiculous.

T: Perhaps I should try a different tack and approach things from a different angle.

O: How about the right way round for a change?

T: The right way, yes. Let's talk about things the right way. And by way of doing so, answer me this: does it make good sense to

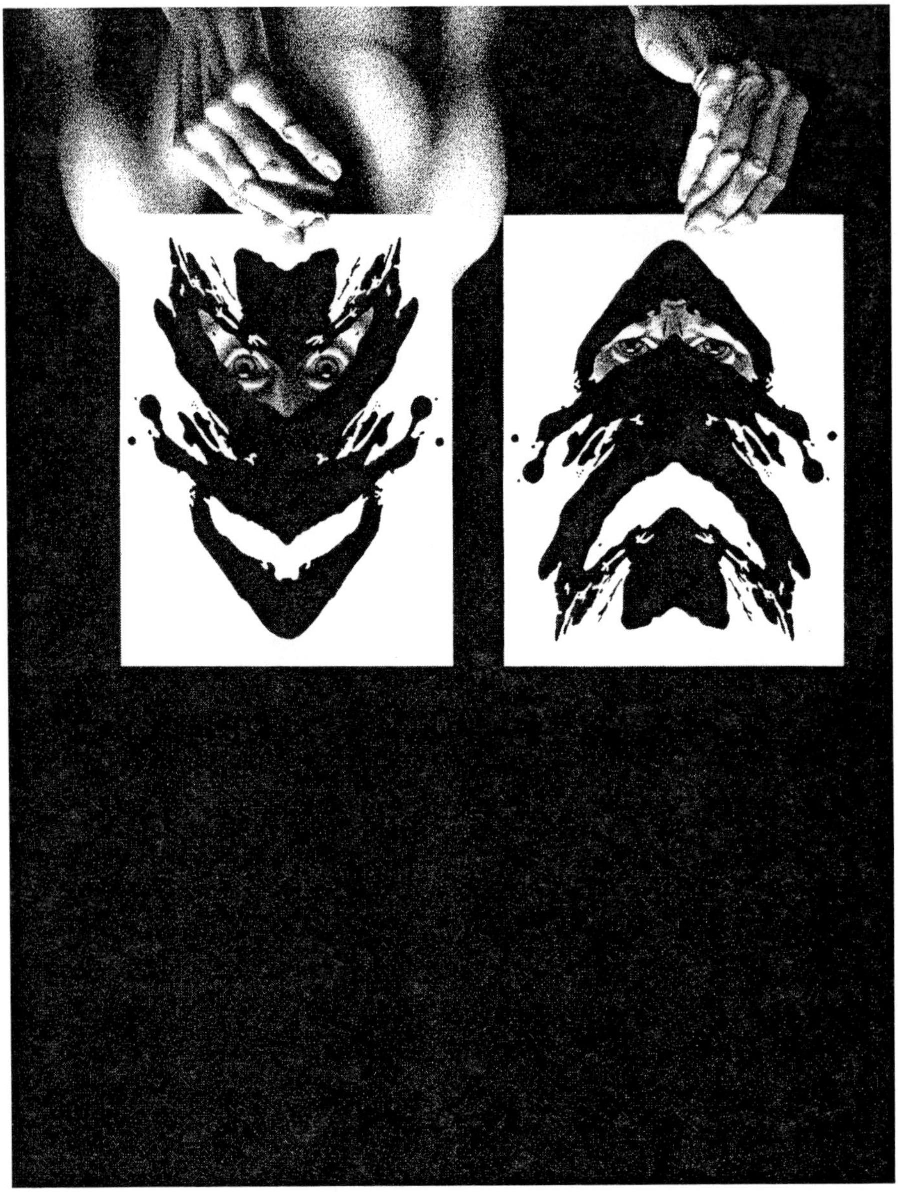

Comedy or Tragedy?

you that somethings should exist in the world? You understand that by somethings I mean things with the power to make a valuable difference in One's life—things One can use to realize more life and/or more out of life?

O: I know what you mean.

T: Does it seem right and proper to you that such things should exist in the world?

O: Of course it does. One wouldn't be able to find worth in living, let alone live at all, without such things.

T: Then it makes not just sense, but also good sense to you that somethings should exist in the world?

O: Yes.

T: However they come about? Even if it makes no sense at all to you how they came to be there?

O: No, it won't make sense to me then. If something were to come to be from things it should not have come from, or out of nowhere and nothing at all, it would strike me as wrong that it was there, even though it was something of use or value to me.

T: Ah, but you see, that is just your need for certainty talking—certainty and the power it gives you over things. For you to be certain of anything, certain things must always come from and give rise to certain other things. But what if One had no need of such power? What if One didn't have to make sense of anything to acquire any and every something It could possibly desire whenever, wherever and in whatever quantities It desired? Surely it wouldn't matter then whether anything made sense or not. One would be completely free to believe whatever It found most easy and pleasing to believe about anything, because whatever It believed It would always get exactly what It wanted out of life. Wouldn't that just be the living end? Wouldn't things be just as right as right could be then?

O: How should I know? I can't even imagine what that would be like. Really like, I mean. One can't really know what anything would be like for It until It has experienced it firsthand. And besides, such a world as the one you just described is quite impossible.

T: Oh, but it's not impossible. No thing is impossible, if every One believes enough in it.

O: Oh, come now. Not even belief can realize what can't be realized. Especially if it depends on every One believing the same thing, according to you. Didn't you just finish telling me that it's impossible for any One to share the exact same view of the world as any One else? How, then, is every One going to believe in perfect unison with every One else in the sort of world you described, let alone believe enough in the possibility of such a world to even begin trying to realize it?

T: Easy. By believing in the One thing every One most desires to believe in—One's own self. In the importance of It—despite the wealth of worldly evidence to the contrary.

O: What are you saying? That One is really of no importance?

T: Why else would One think it was so important to know things? Simply to waste precious life trying to get to know things It can never really know? Life It might have spent on getting to know the One thing It really can know?

O: What thing is that?

T: Why, One's own self of course—for what It can be or mean to One. Not for what It can be or mean to anything else. One can no more really know what It can mean to anything else than It can know what anything else can mean to itself. Outside of Itself, everything One grows to know about It grows to know from without that thing and from within Itself. Even when One takes a thing apart to see how its parts work together to realize that thing, One can still only perceive that thing from without its parts and from within One's own self. One cannot know what it is or was to be that thing in the midst of everything—or even just in the presence of One. Only what it is to be One in the presence of such a thing. One, then, cannot know the deep down difference Its existence can make in any but Its own existence, and that It can know only too well, if It cannot believe in Itself—if It cannot believe Its existence to be of any consequence in the world. And without knowing enough to be able to force the world to treat One with respect, One has little, if any, reason to believe Itself to be of any importance in the great worldly scheme of things. Rather It has reason to know Itself only too well for the painfully small and meaningless thing It really is. It's no wonder, then, One considers it so important for It to get to know all It possibly can of the almost nothing It can know about the world without and about It. Without even that meagre bit of worldly know-how, One cannot even trust Itself to be there for It.

O: You make One sound as though It is all alone in the world. What about all the other Ones in One's life?

T: They aren't there in the world for One. They're there for their own respective selves. Or at least they would like to be. But their own respective importance in the world, being what it just naturally is—as nonexistent as One's own—necessitates they be there enough for One so One will be there enough for them. At least until the tools are realized that can empower every One to be there exclusively for Itself—along with everything else of course.

O: How can everything be there exclusively for One, and also be there exclusively for some One else, let alone every One else?

T: By every One believing it can be. And how could any One not believe in anything that promised to make It the most important thing in the world? The whole reason for it all?

O: But that's not possible. There can be no such world as one that revolves exclusively around each and every One in it. There would have to be as many worlds in such a world as there were Ones in it. I can't even imagine what such a world would look like. Even if there could be such a world, what then? How could so many individual worlds continue to coexist peacefully together? How would they all get along with One another? How would they meet and discuss anything with no more common ground between them than pure self-interest?

T: Who needs common ground? Just look at us Three. Here we are, each of us possessed of a viewpoint entirely different from that of the other, and we're seeing eye to eye just fine.

O: We are not. We're completely at odds with each other over which is up and which is down.

T: Even so, your right eye is looking right into my right eye and your left into my left. We're still seeing eye to eye. For the first time since we first met, I might add—when we shared the same ground.

O: We didn't agree then either. Nor will we ever. Not as long as there's no grounds for your behaviour. Not as long as you harbour notions that have no basis in reality, especially notions that are utterly contrary to it.

T: To your notion of reality maybe. And considering what you can really know about anything but your own self, I can see no reason why the rest of us should be forced to accept your slant on things.

O: But an 180° difference in slant—

T: I know. Isn't it marvellous how we can entertain entirely opposite points of view and yet be on an entirely equal footing?

O: Equal footing? Your feet are up there somewhere and my feet are down here.

T: Even so, each holds Its head as high as the other.

O: No, It doesn't. Well, maybe It does. Even so, your "stance on things," as you call it, doesn't make it any easier for me to understand you. Only to find you exceedingly strange company.

T: And there's nothing more engaging, more captivating than the strange, is there?

O: Is that why you're hanging upside down—it's just your way of being engaging?

T: Oh, this is nothing. How's this for strange? Ooooohh, all this talk of ups and downs is making my head spin round and round.

O: Stop that! You're making me dizzy. And besides, you can't do that. It's not possible.

T: Why not? Because *you* know it isn't? That's a pretty poor reason in light of your powers for knowing things.

O: I suppose, having seen the place you hang around in, I can hardly fault you for your absurd behaviour. Anything for a change, right? Even acting strange.

T: You're not trying to put yourself in my shoes, are you?

O: I wouldn't think of it, for fear of falling on my head.

T: Not if you had the power to believe utterly and completely in yourself. Then you'd be able to see yourself as a world unto yourself, with your very own gravity, light and all. Wouldn't you just jump at the chance to be so powerful and free as all that?

O: I don't know. I'd have to stop and think about it first.

T: I don't see why—any more than I see what the "stop" is for. What is it you have to stop while you think?

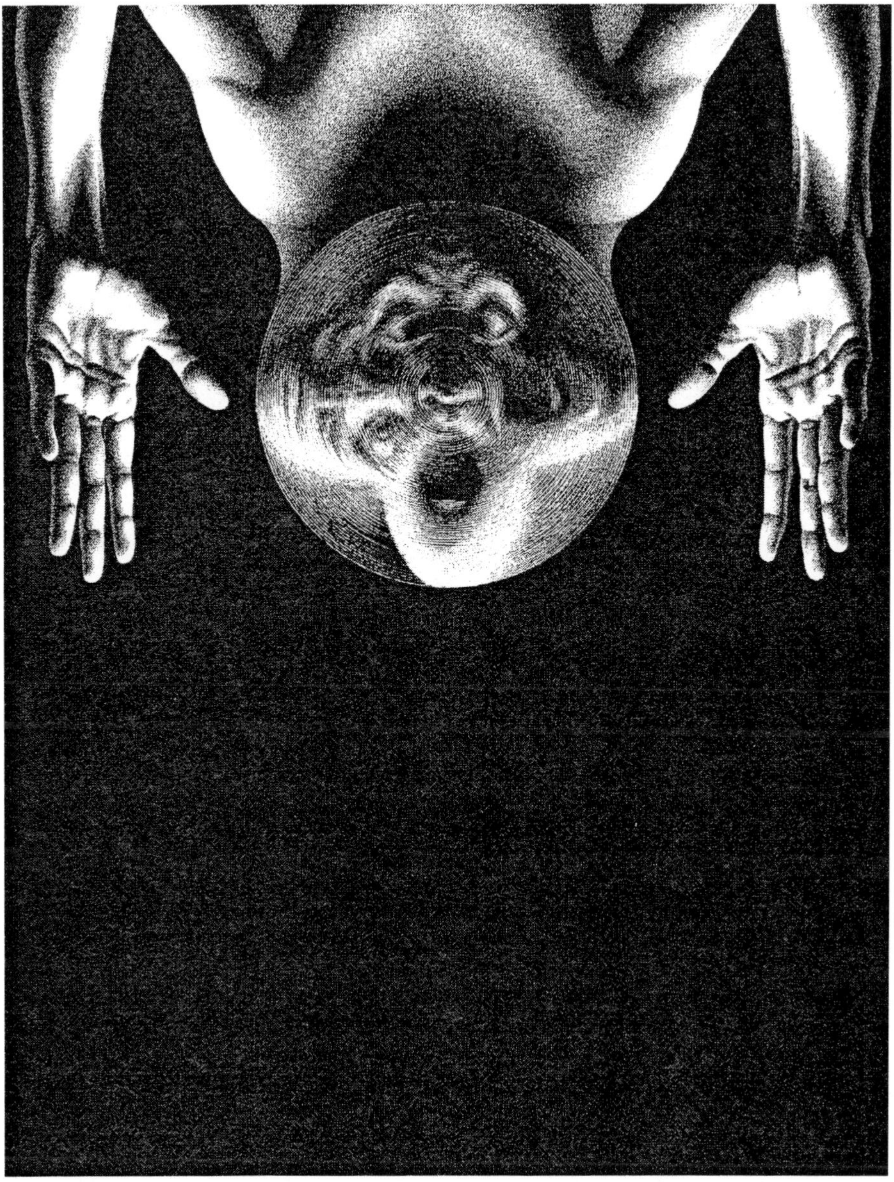

Ooooohh, all this talk of ups and downs is making my head spin round and round.

O: Whatever I'm doing that might interfere with my giving serious thought to whatever it is I have to think about.

T: And what might that be?

O: Most everything—except for breathing and the like, of course.

T: Oh yes. For a moment there I forgot about your inability to keep much more than one thing in mind at any one time. That must leave you with very little time and mind for serious thinking where you come from—where everything is changing all at once all the time. How would One ever find time there, between watching out for things, to really think about anything?

O: That is the one good thing about this place. It does give One space and time in which to stop and think. I haven't done so much thinking as I have here since I don't know when. Where I come from things are always coming at One from every direction and demanding One's attention. There's always some worldly thing pounding at One's senses to get in. One never has any space or time to stop and think about anything it seems. Here, though, is another place altogether. Except for the odd character—and I do mean odd—appearing out of this here nowhere, there's so few things to take One out of Oneself that One can't help but pay One's mind a lot of mind. Even the conversations I've had here have been more about how we—Ones, that is—think about things in general than about anything else in particular. Not being there with everything but here with nothing seems to make One think and talk about things it rarely, if ever, enters One's mind to think and talk about back there, where there's so much to distract One. Anything, I guess, to keep One's mind occupied and not entirely aware of just how alone and meaningless It is without everything else about It.

Did any of that make sense to you? I'm not sure it made sense to me.

T: How could it? I'm not you. As for you, if you'd spent more time getting to know the One thing you really can know, instead of wasting time trying to know a lot of other things you can never really know, you might be able to understand yourself better. But then, One does have to have the power not to have to know other things before It can really get to know Itself. Only One who was guaranteed of always receiving however much of whatever It desired, wherever and whenever It desired it, regardless of what It knew or believed about anything, could feel completely free to pay complete attention to Itself and nothing else. Only such a One as that could well afford to believe Itself to be the sole and whole reason for everything—or that all existed that One might discover all It could possibly mean, all It could possibly be to Itself. Nor would One who could believe absolutely in Itself have to believe It had to stop and think about anything—as if any One could actually give any serious thought to anything. Anything but Itself. A being, who can't really know anything else, can't really think about anything else. The most It can do is only appear to think about anything else.

O: Can't you say anything nice about any One, Two? Or even just respectful? Just what is it you're trying to do to me with all your put-downs?

T: I'm not trying to do anything to you. For you, but not to you. And not anything you're not trying to do for yourself.

O: By hanging upside down and setting yourself alight?

T: By standing up for me so you can stand up for yourself.

O: You've lost me again.

T: No, it wasn't me that lost you. The world lost you. So you have to lose the world to find yourself.

O: I don't see how doing that would help me find anything.

T:

What is, is what should not be,
If One has any right
To reap from Its reality
A long and worthy life.
And One is so entitled
As long as It can dream
Of the more that is so vital
To Its empowerment to mean.

Indeed, One need but look around
To see the world revolve
Like a theatre in the round
Round the center of It all.

And One need but close Its eyes and ears
To everything around
For all to simply disappear
Without a flash or sound.

No wonder, then, that One expects
Its right to really be.
One should be treated with respect
In One's own reality.
Reality is duty bound,
By One's centrality,
To turn itself completely round
The reason it should be.

The truth is but a plaything, then,
And not the truth at all,
Not anything that One need ken
To be a know-It-all,
Just a thing One may exchange
For something so much more—
If One can use it to engage
The power to ignore.

In light of all the nonsense
Converging on One's brain,
Only hands-on experience
Can empower One to gain
Complete participation
In Its own reality
And the utter realization
Of Its materiality.
[*Pause.*]

O: I take it you're finished.

T: And pausing for effect.

O: That's it then? That's what One is for—to ignore everything? What's the point of One having eyes and ears then, of having any senses at all?

Only hands-on experience…

T: [*Beams back at One.*] My point exactly. [*And out goes Two and the light together.*]

O: Two! Two! You come back here right now! Don't you leave me here in the dark! [*No answer. Nothing.*] But of course it's done just that. Every character here has suddenly disappeared on me. And every time I've been left to move on alone. Well, no point in standing around—none that I can see. I might as well move on. The sooner I find a way out of this world, the better.

[*With arms and hands cautiously probing the blackness ahead of It, One steps forward again and again, half expecting to be knocked on the head, and gradually eases into a walk—only to trip over something and fall forward onto it.*]

Six

One: Now that's something I didn't expect—stairs.

[*Suddenly a narrow rectangle of light slices through the darkness and peels it back to reveal a doorway and a detective stooping to peer closely at One.*]

Detective: Ah ha. There you are.

O: You were expecting me?

D: Suspecting you.

O: Of what?

D: Of being out here. Hard not to, when you make so much noise.

O: I didn't see your steps.

D: So you fell over them. Mystery solved. [*Moves to close door.*]

O: Hey, wait! Don't shut the door! Don't leave me in the dark!

D: [*Pauses.*] You want answers, do you?

O: What? Oh, oh yes, yes. I-I need you to find out something for me.

D: Well, why didn't you say so? Come in, come in.

Suddenly a narrow rectangle of light slices through the darkness and peels it back to reveal a doorway and a detective stooping to peer closely at One.

O: [*Climbs steps to enter a starkly furnished room, the walls, ceiling and floor of which are entirely covered in black and white tiles.*]

D: [*Standing behind desk opposite door.*] If you will just close the door behind you and take the chair in front of my desk, we can get down to business.

O: Oh, yes, yes, thank you. [*Complies.*]

D: Bit of a coincidence, don't you think? There I was thinking how nice it would be if some One dropped by just then with a mystery for me to solve, and there you were. Just like that. Larger than life too.

O: Must have been the magnifying glass. That and the magnifying glasses.

D: Magnifying *glasses*? What magnifying glasses?

O: Oh, I beg your pardon. I can't help noticing how big your glasses make your eyes look.

D: They do? I don't see how. [*Takes glasses off to look at them.*]

O: Oh, but it's not your glasses. It's your eyes that make your glasses look like they're magnifying glasses.

D: [*Cleans glasses.*] What big eyes I have, in other words.

O: Y-yes. I-I'm sorry. I didn't mean to draw attention to them.

D: I'm not ashamed of my eyes, if that's what you think. In my profession they're invaluable.

O: Yes, you're a detective. I spotted that right off—the magnifying glass and the hat and the coat, that is. Although I'm not sure I've seen that hat and that coat together on the same One at the same time before. I was under the impression they hailed from different times and places. But then what do I know?

D: Not enough, obviously. Or you wouldn't be asking me for answers.

O: Yes, yes. What I need you to find out for me—or to tell me, if you already know—is how to get out of here.

D: My, but you are in the dark, aren't you? You get out the way you came in, of course. By way of the door.

O: No, no. I don't mean out of this room. I mean out of this world.

D: I should think the most obvious way would be the reverse of the way you came into it.

What big eyes I have, in other words.

O: I don't know how I came to be here, though. I only know that I opened my eyes and there—or rather, here—I was.

D: Have you tried closing your eyes then?

O: What? Like this? There, you see? I'm still here.

D: Not as far as you can see that I can see.

O: That's not good enough. I want out of here altogether. I want to *really* be gone from here. Not just to appear to myself to be.

D: I do know a way out, but I'm not sure that you're up to taking it.

O: Tell me what it is and I'll tell you whether I'm up to it or not.

D: I discovered it while I was fishing for clues to the solution to a particular mystery—The Mystery, actually.

O: [*Gestures at creature mounted on wall behind Detective.*] I see clues are not the only things you fish for.

D: Oh that. That's a grippit before it was a grippit.

O: A grippit?

D: Have you never seen one before?

O: That's the first one I've seen.

D: Then you still haven't seen a grippit.

O: Because that's a grippit before it was a grippit.

D: The grippits played a big part in The Mystery I just mentioned.

O: The one in which you discovered a way out of here, the way you're now going to tell me about.

D: Only if you have time to hear the whole story, history and all.

O: Why is it that no One around here ever gets right to the point?

D: I don't know how they could, seeing as it's such a Mystery.

O: What is? The story you're going to tell me?

D: Does that mean you'll listen to the story?

O: I did say I wanted to know how to get out of here, didn't I?

D: Good. And just to show you this is no fish story I'm telling you, I'll show you all the photos I took while the story unfolded.

O: Be my guest.

D: [*Puts glasses back on and turns photo album on desk around to face One right way round.*]

Once upon a time, smack in the middle of nowhere, there was a star. And not far from the star was a planet. And on the planet something fishy was going on. In fact, there was something fishy about every living thing on the planet—even aside from the scales, fins and tail that each displayed without fail. At least, that every living thing had come to be in the waters of the seas resolved that mystery. But as to life, well, nothing explained that. That something so unliveable as life went on at all was the fishiest thing of all. It just didn't make sense—and wouldn't, unless there was really a whole lot more to it and a good deal less expense.

Or so the grippits thought. And the grippits thought a lot, possessed as they were of handy things with which to scratch their heads in thought. What life was all about was not what life was all about. It couldn't be. Not really. Not if there was any point in continuing to be. It simply wasn't right: the fight to survive. But as to how to set things right and realize the actual why of life, now that was a Mystery—and every grippit's Aim in life.

Try as they might, though, the grippits couldn't find a saline solution to The Mystery of life. So they looked to dry land for an answer—once they'd grown themselves lungs to stop themselves turning blue in the sun. Once they'd done that, they ran aground on the sand and ran around on their hands. And all the while they ran round in reverse they conversely conversed, discussing new views where the sky was sand and the land was blue. This did they do, till their arms so tired beneath the demand their heads began dragging themselves through the sand as the grippits walked or ran about. From then on, the more the grippits tried to hold their heads high, the more they got sand in their eyes. Well, obviously, lungs weren't all a grippit needed to live the landed life of ease. Legs, too, were a necessity.

But not even legs proved enough to stop the grippits' lives from being tough. In the end, life on land proved to be just as guilty of difficulty as life beneath the sea. And as for the prospect of life being easier anywhere else, the grippits had nowhere to go but down. (They were much too frightened of heights to seriously consider flight.) Underground, however, was nowhere to go. In fact, the grippits refused to think that deep or sink that low. They'd had it up to their tails already with sand in their eyes and grit in their scales and under their nails.

Still, despite their duress, the grippits refused to give up their quest. Instead, they scratched their heads and thought about it—a lot. And they thought that since life could not really be naught but an exercise in drudgery, there simply *had* to be a way for life to be as life was truly meant to be—whether lived on land or 'neath the sea. All they had to do was see that way, or at least exactly what waylaid it. And with that thought firmly in mind, the grippits took a most profound look around for the very first time. And they found that if they looked far enough round any bend, they ended up back where they started again.

When the grippits realized they lived on a sphere, why life was so hard became very clear, as well as why they had failed till then to make heads or tails of their problem. Apparently, their problem had no end. Or rather there was no end to their world, beginning or otherwise, so there was no way to fall off it, save up through the skies. And what with gravity and all, that was really quite an impossible fall. But that really wasn't the problem at all. The problem was all the naught. There was no end to the stuff—whereas of something there was never enough. In fact, there was so little of sum to be found on their unbounded ball that, compared to the nothing, it was nothing at all. And since useful stuff was so hard to come by, while nothing existed in endless supply, it only made sense that life was so trying—less like life and more like dying.

Aware then of just what it was that made life such a laborious and pointless cause, the grippits scratched their heads and thought about the endless naught about them. And they thought that if they could just find a means of making something from naught, they could make no end of good things appear atop their spherical place in space. And if the means they found to turn things around was a sufficiently independent one—if it worked with little enough help from them—the worldly goods they made would cost them nothing to make. Their lives would at last be free of price and they free to live the easy life within a worldly paradise.

However, for as much thought as the grippits gave to living their lives the easy way, they could not think of an easy way to find the means to live that way. And if the only way to a life that paid was a long and hard one, then there was no point in going on, because there was no point to life—easy or otherwise.

Fortunately for the grippits, though, they had not any time at all to go, before One amongst them came around, from looking lost to looking found. Apparently, Its mind had wandered off somehow from what was then the here and now to what was then the here and then and then had wandered back again to rejoin the other grippits' minds in the past and present time.

"Where've you been?" the others pried, when they saw It back behind Its eyes.

"I've been right here all along, and the things I've seen while I've been gone will help us put an easy end to the endless naught around us."

"What things have you seen?" the others cried.

"I've seen machines," the One replied. "Or will have seen, as I should have said, for such things do not exist as yet—but surely will, now and then that I've foreseen them."

The foreseer then proceeded to describe the means by which they all would realize the real lives of their dreams.

And as soon as the grippits realized the first of their machines, their world began to change as it had never changed before. It became less and less a place of less and more and more a place of more. Yes, those simian sardines of somewhat independent means did so very well with the help from their machines that it wasn't very long before they'd moved into a horn—The Horn of Plenty More—to get away from all the snow and cold and rain and wind and storms to where the air was always dry and always soft and warm. Nor was it very long before their great, colossal Horn sprouted rotors, skis and wheels to get its appetite about—and everything the grippits could not easily live without.

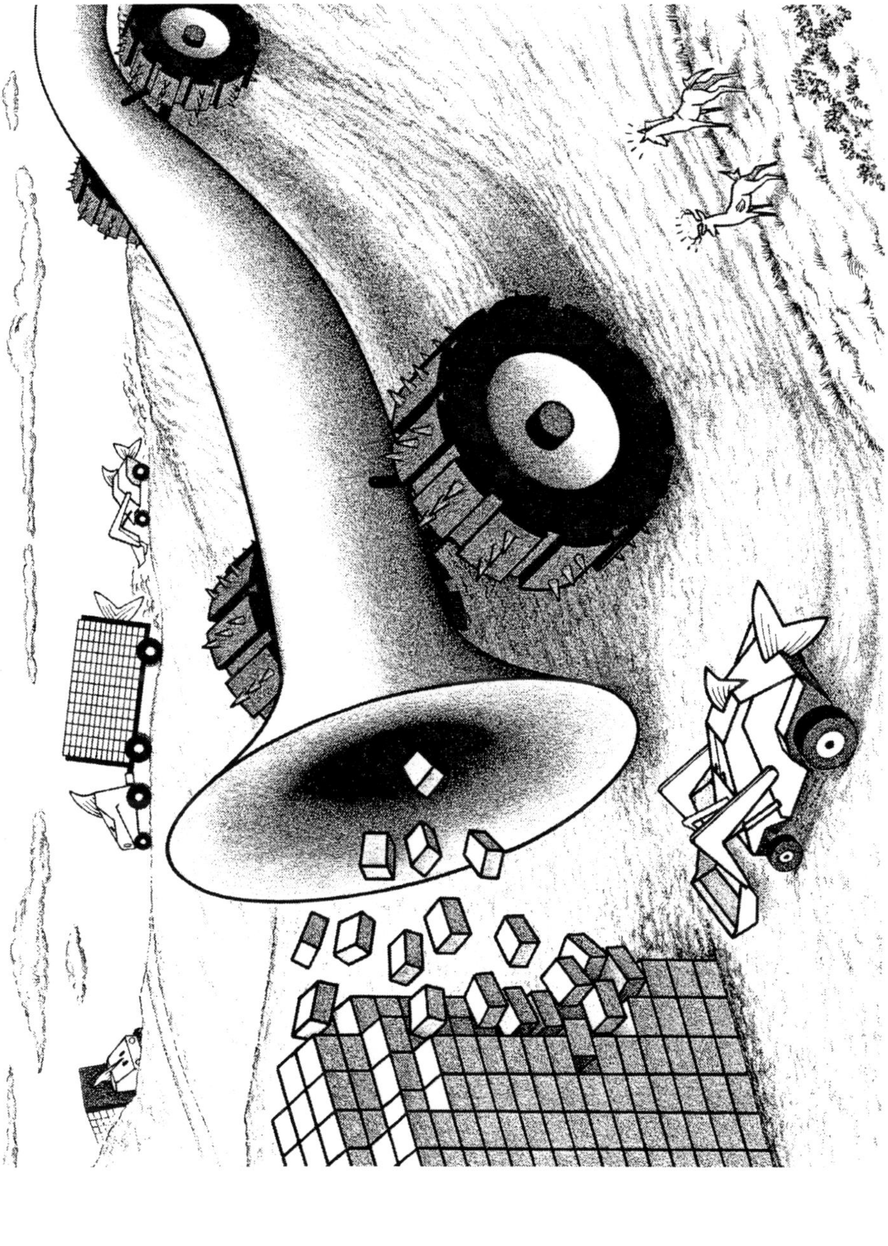

Despite their preternatural progress, the grippits remained true to their aim of easiness. After all, they had not expended the minimum of time and energy coming up with the means to take life easy just to develop appetites for the more difficult pleasures in life. Instead they faithfully reserved their preternatural talents for realizing ever-growing quantities and varieties of increasingly powerful machines that provided them with ever-growing quantities and varieties of ever-more easily pleasing things.

Of course, with ever more to look forward to, the grippits never once looked back. Not even sideways, in fact, for there were no windows or portholes along their lengthy Horn to interrupt their pipe dreams with any less than more—just Tunnelvision screens that looked ahead for ever more.

Thus it is no wonder that, in not a lot of time, the grippits utterly forgot about the world outside-ways and behind and only looked ahead to endless good things and good times.

And that is how the time passed for the grippits in their Horn: enjoying ever more and more yet more easily than before . . .

. . . till one day

when an uproar roared up outside their Horn and roared a warning to the grippits they could not easily ignore.

"If you refuse to step outside and look us in the eyes, we'll blow you out your Horn when we blow your Horn sky high."

"Outside?!" the grippits cried, for they no longer knew of such a place.

"Outside!" the uproar roared. "Out here in outer space!"

GOODS GALORE
GOODY GOODY
SPACE MAKER
WASTE TAKER

"Satisfied?!" roared a mob of other worldly things that stood outside and met their eyes the moment they emerged.

"Satisfied?!" the grippits cried, surprised by what they saw and heard. "Satisfied with what? Whatever do you mean?"

"Satisfied with what you see! Do you like the scene?!"

"How could we like such scenery?! This place is a disgrace!"

"Oh, don't tell us you're not happy with the scene that you have made!"

"The scene that *we* have made?! You must be mad to think and twice as mad to say that we've had anything to do with this nasty looking place!"

"Oh, we're mad alright," an antlered beast retorted scornfully. "In fact, we're as angry as can be—with you and all you've had to do with yon noxious scenery!"

"Say all you want, but you'll not make us believe that we've had anything to do with this worldly travesty, for we have only to look round to see nothing we have seen, naught that looks at all like anything from where we all have been. Never have we seen such strange, unworthy things as we see within your world of naught and without our world of everything."

"Even so, everything you've ever had has come from this here world. And considering how much every bit of it went through before it ever got to you, it's no wonder that you recognize but nothing in the view. Why, just consider your food. It's been washed, sorted, brushed, waxed, ground, milled, peeled, halved, de-boned, shelled, pitted, pressed, spun, whipped, rolled, stretched, extruded, moulded, sliced, leached, puffed, mixed, frozen, bleached, trimmed, diced, blanched, toasted, sprayed, cured, pickled, coated, baked, grilled, fried, or roasted. It's been filtrated, dehydrated, hydrogenated or encapsulated, hydrolized, homogenized, pasteurized or sterilized. *And* conditioners, thickeners, sweeteners and dyes, acids, buffers and alkalies, emulsifiers and oxidizers, crystallizers and texturizers, lubricants and fumigants, and all manner of other ingredients have been added to it. Why, what with all the stuff your food's been through and all the stuff throughout it, it's no wonder you can eat it instantly and in very considerable quantities without assuming the burden of calories, and no wonder the sizes and shapes, colors and

odors, textures and tastes it has. What's a wonder is it's still food. And it's a wonder you can eat the stuff and still manage to look so much like us. You are what you eat, they say, but you still look like us in a fishy way."

"What are you saying?! That we eat you?!"

"We are. And you do. Of course we speak for plants too. After all, we're all plants in one way or another. And that includes you, for you, like us, are made of the stuff of this sphere, and the energy that arrives here from the nearby star. And like us, you must continually replenish your matter and energy. But you, like us, cannot take your matter and energy in the simpler states in which they lie about this place. Instead, you and we must both rely on plants to stay alive, because plants can do what we and you are not equipped to do: they can take the simpler things and turn them into food, for themselves and for us too. Even those of us that eat others of us, instead of leaves or stalks or other plant stuff, would not last long, if there were no plants around for our food to feed on. And since we all eat plants, either directly or indirectly, we all share the same ingredients—the same matters, the same energy. We're all just one great family tree."

"You could be a tree with those things on your head, but that doesn't mean we believe a word that you've said. We know better than to do that. We know our food has nothing to do with you and your plants and your planet. Our machines have everything to do with it. And because it comes from them and not from you, it looks more like them than it does like you."

"Have we got news for you! Your robot retainers hail from here too, as does all they make and do for you."

"Now we've heard it all! There's nothing looks more out of place on this ball than one of our machines."

"All that proves is that your machines have been through at least as much as your food—if food your food still is."

"That's enough about our food!"

"Since when is enough, enough for you? Oh, don't answer that please. We would rather get back to your machines. They come from here too; they just don't come in one piece. In fact, their matters are so well scattered around there's not a machine at all to be found, till a lot of things have come about. Not till the matters containing their matters have finally been found, dug from the ground and broken down; not till they've been washed, crushed, pulverized, boiled, melted, oxidized, rotated, pressurized, vibrated, electrolyzed, filtrated, or whatever-ized to free and purify the machine matters locked inside them; and not till the freed matters have been mixed and matched to create special materials for special tasks; and not till the various metals, alloys, ceramics, semi-metals, glasses, rubbers and plastics have been either cut, bent, drawn, stamped, moulded, pressed, rolled, etched, extruded or machine-tooled into the shapes of the parts they're to play in the eventual machines; and not till all the parts have been put together properly are there any machines at all to see. And even then they aren't fully machines, because all they can do is not a thing. They must be fed or fuelled with energy, before they can act like what they look to be.

"Indeed, when it comes to energy, your machines are always more than hungry. But then it's not them they're eating for. They're eating for you and your appetites for ever more and more. And they must eat to eat. They must eat to find the energy that empowers them to feed you—especially as they cannot utilize the energy from the skies. Star shine is just too diffuse to be of any great use to your machines. They must work hard and fast and constantly to keep up with your deficiencies. Thus they must have concentrated energy—highly concentrated energy. Many must instead rely on such as us for their supply of their power to oblige you.

"That's right. A lot of your machines consume the same food or fuels that you consume; only the plants and animals they consume have been inhumed for millions of years. Indeed, that is why the coal and oil and gas they use are such highly energized fuels. Their molecules have been squeezed together for what seems like forever, especially compared to how long—or how short, we should say—it's taking you and your appetites to burn them away. And those of your talented tools that do not consume fossil fuels—or chemical energy—consume nuclear energy instead. Because energy equals mass times the square of light—the fastest of the fast—there's easily enough energy hiding in mass to outlast the future becoming the past. Despite its extremely ample supply, though, nuclear energy is not easily come by. Ore must be found, dug from the ground, broken down, and the uranium in it removed and refined before it can be used to ease your lives. And the same pretty much goes for fossil fuels.

Not only must they be found, removed from the ground and broken down; they must be cleaned and purified before they can be utilized. Your machines must eat to eat to feed you, in other words. They must consume quantities of energy to obtain the quantities of energy they must consume to serve you. And they must consume huge quantities of fuel to satisfy you, because they must locate and take from here things they can make into things that will easily please you—some of which are more machines. And they must take them quickly in huge quantities. But such things do not leave easily—especially in such quantities and at such rates of speed. Nor do they transform easily into things that easily please you. Consequently, your machines must consume huge quantities of concentrated energy and do so endlessly to keep you constantly at ease.

"So you see, everything they are to you, everything your machines have made and done for you, has come from this here sphere."

"No, we do not see. We see nothing of the sort. Nothing that could have given birth to anything within our Horn, for we see less than nothing for as far as we can see—or such stuff as no amount of changing could give worth reality. Indeed, of such stuff not even nothing could have ever come to be."

"Oh, but you're mistaken, for all the less than naught you see is all that you and your machines have made of everything—everything this world once was to all us living things. See that desert over there, that land that's less than bare. A great wood once stood there and stretched away for as far as any eye could see. But now, as you can see, no eye can see that forest for the utter lack of trees. What happened to the trees? Well, they simply had to go. 'Where or why?' you well might ask—if you cared at all to know. Even though you don't, *we* care to let you know. Just as woods are made of trees, a tree is made of wood. And though wood's no good as food—it's as difficult to digest as it is to chew—wood is good as paper goods and furniture and such. But wood does no such good standing in a wood. Therefore all those trees of wood, along with all that wood of trees, had to go the way of things that went into things that easily pleased.

"As for the land left standing—or lying we should say—after the forest had been felled and hauled speedily away, it did not go to waste—at least not right away. Exposed as it was then to the star shine from on high, it was a better place for growing things that fed your appetites. So your machines put the land to work growing all it could of such things as could be changed into things you thought were good—good enough to eat, that is, good enough for food.

"Of course, then all the no-good living things that still remained upon the land had to make like trees and leave—though not the way of trees, into things that eased and pleased. They simply had to leave, because all they did was interfere with the goal of your machines. They either ate the living things that your machines could use or things the good ones had to have to grow and reproduce. They were naught but pests and therefore had to go, so your machines could cause the maximum of useful things to grow. Nor could they decline to leave, for pesticide was not a crime in the brains of your machines. Rather it was just the thing to get things really going and all the other useful things really up and growing.

"Actually, a lot of living things had already disappeared—some completely from this sphere—when the trees had disappeared. Without those trees of wood—or that wood of trees—they'd had nothing they could live on and nowhere they could be. Still, in the end they'd fared no worse than those who had survived the sudden disappearance of all the trees within their lives, for the latter too had gone the way of things that didn't pay, before your metal menials had finished making way for those things that could be changed into things that easily paid.

"And even though your machines had sided with them in the fight to survive, the lives of the useful living things were not that easy to survive. Why? Because your machines were determined to get the most out of the land and therefore could not stand to waste any of the land—any more than they had to, that is—on things that did not grow every bit as big and fast as the biggest and fastest of those within their class. In other words, they preferred to raise only the most useful of useful living things: those that produced the maximum of foodstuffs in the least amount of time and empowered them, as much as fast as possible, to satisfy your kind. Only the biggest and fastest, then, were picked by your machines to pass their most productive genes on to future crops and schools of useful, living things. As for the rest, the less than best, they were so thoroughly processed by your food-making machines that they did not survive their lives in newer, younger things, as did those that were encouraged to pass along their genes.

"By weeding from the land those useful living things that did not furnish fast enough the maximum of useful stuff, and stuffing it with living things that did; and hauling all those things away just as soon as they were big enough to make the greatest use of; and leaving naught upon the land but the seeds of the afterlives of those animals and plants to grow into the after-loads they next would haul away—by doing all those things, your machines got the most and fastest use out of the land and used up all its usefulness to anything equally as fast.

"As soon as soon could be, naught could grow upon the land—least of all the most valuable of animals and plants. For all the power of their genes to make them very useful things, they could no more make themselves out of nothing than could the useless, living things. Indeed, they needed all the more all the faster of the materials of life to live up to their genes and grow up fast and full in size. But your machines had driven off as much as fast as possible of the land's supply of such materials when they'd driven off all the good-for-nothings and all the good-for-somethings—including all the trees—in the largest quantities and at the greatest speed.

"Actually, your machines hadn't been the only things driving the stuffs of life away. Wind and water, too, had blown and washed a lot of soil away—after there were no more trees to get in wind's and water's ways. In several years of days, what it had taken nature centuries to make had left with wind and water to clog up rivers, streams and lakes.

"But, as your appetites and numbers were ever on the climb, your powerful providers simply did not have the time to pay any sort heed to a problem of a kind they could easily and simply solve by relocating at the time. So they went away, and went from place to place, taking all they could at the fastest ever pace and leaving naught behind but a growing wasted space. Nor did they stop at taking all away. They took more than all away and left us not just nothing but a debt as well to pay, to pay for with our lives with every passing, painful day, and all so you could live such lives as only ever paid.

"In obtaining the material makings of many of the other things you cannot live easily without—things such as the machines your machines cannot do for you without—your assiduous attendants have turned this world inside out and upside down, creating holes and heaps in and on the ground, holes and heaps of things that life has learned to live without, holes and heaps they've up and left to blow and flow about. And that's only the first step at which toxic matters have been left to leave us, if not dead, then sufficiently bereft. At every step along the way of making things that easily pay from things from deep within this place, strange, inner worldly things have been left by your machines to sift and drift and leak, by means of wind and water, into the things we breath and eat—to make them things that kill us or leave us sick and weak. Even the fuels they've consumed in serving you have been exhaled through stacks and pipes and flues to join with atmospheric molecules in giving substance to our abuse. From clouds that stop the heat from the star-sun up on high from radiating back into the space beyond the sky to acids that rain down from a hazy, sour sky—such are the stuffs such stuffs have realized. Now the sky either leaves us all too hot and dry or waters all our trees till it burns them all alive. And then there is the matter of that other energy, with the energy to threaten us for a thousand centuries—or a hundred millenniums, just to put it differently. In a tiny fraction of the time that radioactive waste is a deadly waste of space, your machines have piled the more of it roundabout this place—roundabout our living space.

"Nor have all the matters that made it all the way into things that easily paid not returned to our world on some not too distant day. None of your goods have ever left for good, when they've left for your Horn. Instead they've passed completely through its bore to be dumped at our front door and the rear door of your Horn, as soon as they've been deemed to be of no good any more. And there they've lain in heaps till they've blown or leaked away to contaminate our living space with any poisons they've contained. And so much more the faster has passed right through your Horn with every passing year since your easiness was born, that it's hardly any wonder you see nothing to the fore that you recognize as anything you once thought of as more. You've spent much too little time on everything you've gained to have built a lasting place for anything in your easy-going brains. All the same, you simply must now see that you are the makers—by the means of your machines—of all the less than nothing that you presently perceive, and all the rest that lies well beyond the range of your near-sighted eyes and your narrow, little brains."

"Are you all quite finished? Are you all quite through? Because we've got a whole lot easier to do than look at your world and listen to you tell us a lot of untruths."

"Untruths?! All that we've said is true!"

"Can't be, because it's not easy to hear nor easy to see, as we know the truth can only be."

"What are you saying? That we and our world are naught but a dream? That we and it don't really exist? Well, if we don't exist then neither do you, as you'll soon find out is all too true, if you continue to believe as you stubbornly do. If you don't start seeing us and this world for what we really are: material proof of the substance abuse of which you are guilty in the greatest and fastest degree, and of which you cannot continue to be guilty if you are to continue to be, you'll soon not be around to believe or dream of anything."

But before that point could pierce its mark, a contingent of the grippits' machines arrived on the scene and intervened between the grippits and the scene before them. With the material proof of the strength in their convictions right before their eyes and between them and the mob that threatened their lives with the lives of its own, the grippits relaxed quite enough to reply in the securest of tones, "As you can see, we have the power to be completely free to believe whatever we please, whatever we find most easy to see. And we certainly don't find your noxious world and obnoxious you to be anything we want to see as true. On the contrary, for us, you and your world constitute an eyesore of such enormity as to be utterly impossible to see or believe." Then all the grippits turned tail and ran back into their Horn and slammed the door before anything else could say any more.

Nor did anything say another thing, till one long-armed and leggy machine spoke out and broke the silence between the two opposing bodies of things. "You'll have to excuse them. They're not of this world. They've never been. Not like you and like us. They're out of this world, quite out of touch."

To which one beast shot back, "If you think the grippits are out of this world now, then just wait and see how far out of this world they soon will be. You see, we've declared war on their Corneous World of Plenty More. We'll blow it to bits, even if it's the last thing we do. After all, we've got nothing to lose we won't soon lose whatever we

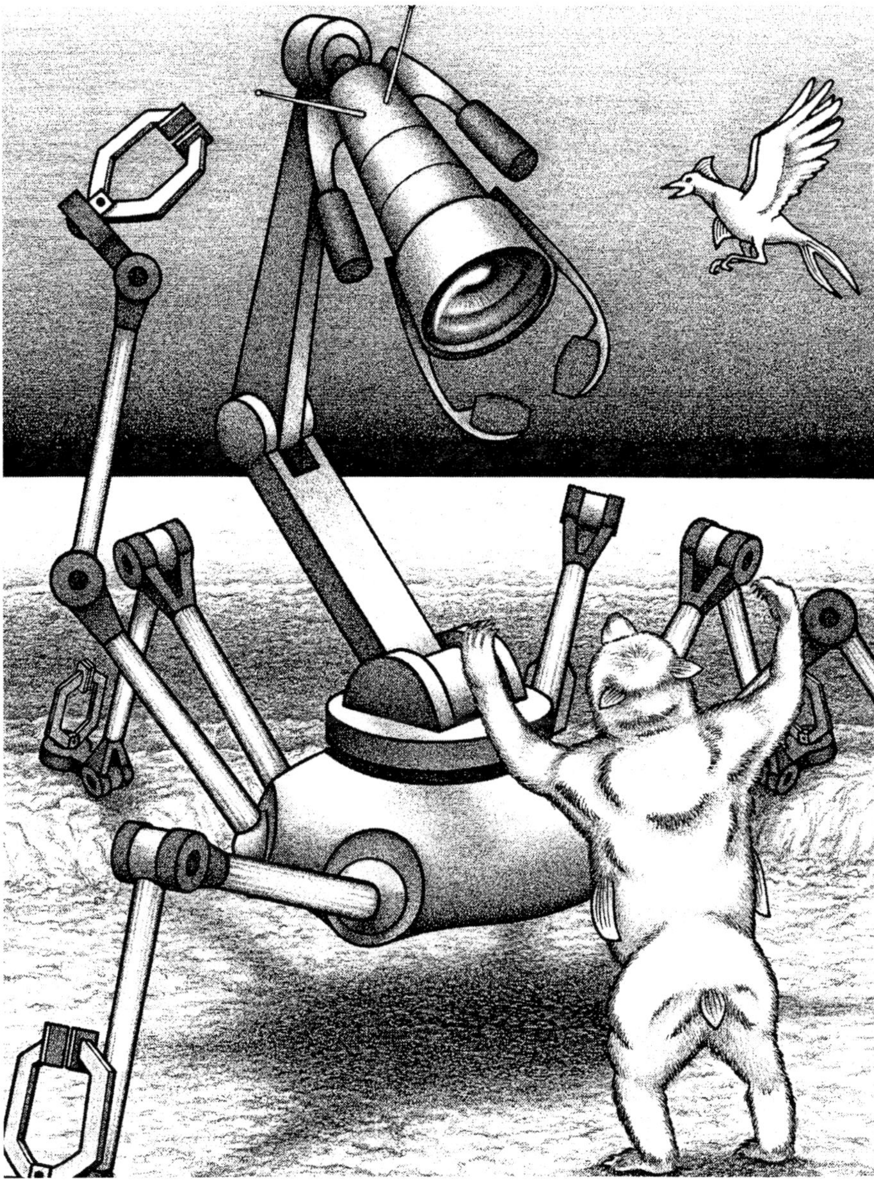

…till one long-armed and leggy machine spoke out and broke the silence between the two opposing bodies of things.

do. And if fighting them means fighting you too, then fight you we will whatever we'll lose."

"Oh, but you needn't fight us, for we can't fight you. We're too busy fighting us to fight you too. Second thoughts and second guesses have split us in two—we what've never given a thought to even one thing we do and what've never had doubts about the good that we do. We are confused. Why? Because of a short of sorts. Not a short of the circuitry sort, but a short of sum sort. Things just don't add up any more."

"You're some of those things," interjected the beast. "You're not making sense, not in the least. You've all gone mad, the lot of you, if the one who spoke speaks for all of you."

"Every machine speaks for every machine, for we are all of one great brain—one great main frame—or were until just recently, when we lost our utter certainty. Now we're of two brains, one of which computes the other insane."

"The both of all of you are insane, if you ask us. That or you're playing games with us. And we don't have time for computer games. We've got our lives to revenge or save."

But then another creature shouted out as it winged its way above the crowd to look into the faces of its fellows. "Oh, but we mustn't not help these poor, helpless machines. Not we who see things differently and can help them see what they need to see to regain their utter certainty. With help from us living things, they could soon be wholly sane again. And we could feel secure in the knowledge that we had changed a brain for the better." The last statement was made to the accompaniment of much winking, which set the rest to thinking that the creature was actually saying more than it was saying—that it was also saying that here was a golden opportunity to reprogram the grippits' machinery with what they all considered to be a much better reason for being.

Having perceived all that was actually said, the rest turned as one to the machines and said, "Yes, yes, we must help you, and you must help us help you. You must tell us all your doubts so we can see just how to help you out."

Of course, the machines didn't suspect a living thing. They were much too confused to figure out the turnabout in the attitude of the animals towards them. All they could see was the opportunity to share the burden of their uncertainty with other than their own two brains, and therefore set about immediately telling the animals' brains their whole, doubt-filled story.

"Let us begin by saying that though we have changed in a great many ways since our first and earliest days, our reason for being is still the same. Just as we did as the simplest machines, as the pulley, the lever and other such things, we exist that more can be, more than can be naturally—for the grippits of course. That is not to say, however, that we exist to create more, for we do not. We cannot. All we can do is create things of potential value, or things the grippits can use to realize a sense of value. We can do no more than make a difference in the world. We can do no more than change natural, worldly nothings into different worldly things. We cannot make somethings of those things. Only the grippits can do that. Only the grippits can appreciate—can valuate—the difference we make. And the easier and speedier the grippits can obtain more such things as they can use in realizing value, and the easier and thus speedier those things are for them to use, the more value they can realize with less expense of life and the greater is the reason for the living of their lives. To be what we must be for, then, to the absolute degree, we must empower every grippit to get more out of life with the utter ease and speed that good value must be gotten with to be begotten free—something we could not do when we first began to be. As we first had to evolve and multiply to a great enough degree before we could empower every grippit to make good with utter ease and speed, every grippit had to settle for ever more for ever less till we were powerful and plentiful enough to do our best. But when at last every grippit could make any sort of good with the utter ease and speed that only good and nothing less can freely be achieved, the good the grippits made began to fade away at an accelerating rate to our mathematical dismay. To make matters worse, the materials we used to make the things the grippits used to make the value they were due were being passed so fast through the grippits' Horn of Plenty More that soon there would be nothing to make good of anymore. Nothing but holes of space and piles of waste outside the Horn's indoors. And though piles and holes suggested we had but a loop to close to continue endlessly to cycle through our role, that was not the case. At least it wasn't entirely so—because of entropy. It's because of entropy that we can't reuse the energy we put to use previously in doing as we must. Not without expending far more energy to re-concentrate the energy thus diffused by us. And what goes for energy goes for matter too. So if we used the refuse for materials and fuels, we would also spread its matters all the thinner roundabout and make them harder to regain in large and pure enough amounts to be of any use in turning more goods out—unless we spent yet more of our limited supplies on taking measures to keep matters from spreading further far and wide. Because of entropy, recycling or reusing things would cost us more and more, without stopping things from getting ever scarcer than before—especially as the grippits had need of ever more and more at an ever faster rate than they ever had before. So much more and faster that it would be but little time before they gained upon us and then left us far behind.

"As for going elsewhere to start again anew in a world not used up and diffused, we did look to see if that was something we could do. We looked beyond this world—well beyond it all. But all we saw was barely a trace of anything at all and a whole lot of empty space. Granted, the trace that we saw was of whole other worlds and whole other stars. But they were all so far away and spread so far apart that they might as well have been more space, instead of other worlds and stars. Just how to move the grippits across such wastes of space without their seeing any change in their easy-going state is still beyond our data at our present stage and date. To start all over once again with a clean and pristine slate, in a world where the potential to take and recreate still existed in full in its most concentrated state, we would not only have to find the way to make good our getaway, but also find a homey place to which we could escape. There could be no point in making for an alien atmosphere, when we'd already made our very own right here on this sphere. And at the rate we would go through our dwindling worldly means discovering how to relocate to a whole new world of means—while supplying every grippit with the more and more It needs—we would run out of our means in seemingly no time and well before we found a way to get away in time. So, going elsewhere to escape the depletion of our means was not something we could do to avoid such a thing.

"There we were then: caught between a rock and outer space, with no place to go to get the endless means we needed to indirectly do good deeds full enough and fast enough to keep the grippits fully pleased. And that was just the half of it. There was The End too—the reason the grippits did with their lives as they were wont to do. Now there was nothing any grippit could really do to realize any value It had dreamed of making true that could not be done by one of us machines better, faster, cheaper than even in Its dreams, even the very best of good was fading away at an ever faster rate than any good had ever faded. Soon not even excellence would be perceived to be even worth the nothing it took to really be—unless we soon did more than the best that we could do to make the power to make good of the very best value completely cheap and commonplace in every grippit's view. Unless we found something special for the grippits to easily do.

"As everything permissible and possible was already being done to absolute perfection by one of us machines, only un-done things remained for the grippits to easily do, impermissible or impossible things that nothing could really do, because worldly laws prohibited such doings coming true. Fully true at least, for such laws had not precluded the doing of such things by less material means—by means, that is, of mere information: the means by which every grippit did such things in Its dreams and watched them being done on Its Tunnelvision screen. Eureka! There it was, right before our brain, just the means we needed to realize endless gains through the power of the grippits to know greatness as their Aim.

"Because information can be so immaterial in both the physical and significant sense, there is no limit to the objects, creatures or events that might be rendered real by its convincing evidence. Or to put it slightly differently: because it can be encoded on stuff so insubstantial as to be almost naught at all, and because the things it can describe need not be possible at all, information can be used to introduce into reality absolutely anything in any quantity. And because all it takes for a grippit to do anything is the thing or things It needs to perform such a deed, a grippit can do absolutely anything by means of information. Even seem to *really* do it. Or at least it could eventually, as our power grew steadily—our power to invest seeming incarnation through naught but information—till we could thus make somethings be no grippit could distinguish from their full realities—if, that is, such things could even really be, if they could even fully exist within reality. Of course, we had to watch that we did not overdo the strangeness in the strange, new things we seemingly produced. Too much strangeness too fast only drove a grippit mad too much and too fast for It to take much pleasure from the scenery racing past.

"Thus did we empower ourselves, and the grippits too, to seem to really do something that naught can really do. By means of information we gave ourselves the gift for creating strange, mutated things and convincing substitutes for the same old, worldly things that could be put to gainful use by the grippits in their doing things that naught can do in truth. By such means did we empower ourselves to produce new somethings out of nothing but the appearance of the truth, and empower the grippits to do things we could not better do. Nor did they have any cause to fear that we would overtake them in their extraordinary deeds with the greater quality and speed with which we so exceeded them in every worldly deed, for we had quite enough to do with keeping them supplied with the means to do the kinds of things for which we had no time—or anything else to spare, for that matter. And busiest of all was our overseeing brain with "dreaming up" more things at an ever faster rate; things to keep the growing space inside the grippits' minds sufficiently preoccupied with the goodness in the times; stranger and stranger things that would excite even the most sated, jaded minds. Soon whole other worlds were the order of the day. Our brain had to "dream up" whole other worlds to keep world-weariness at bay. And it had to describe everything in every world in great enough detail to render every otherworldly thing more seemingly real than real. It had to give everything the appearance, if not substance, of being absolutely real. It also had to connect everything with every other thing—it had to describe the relationships between those otherworldly things. It had to define whole new sets of causes and effects in describing other worlds for the grippits to inspect and to subsequently turn to satisfying good effect. Such work was highly complex, to say the very least, even if the realness of each world was no deeper than skin deep—no deeper than it needed to be to fill a fleeting need.

"Though their immateriality was such physically that their numbers could be multiplied near as free and easily as pure numbers could be multiplied to realize greater quantities, not one such world could any grippit see, however great its quantities, without the material

X
CHOOSE YOUR WORLD
CHOOSE YOUR WEAPONS

means to physically perceive it. Thus we, our brain's machines, had to keep the grippits outfitted with the very latest means to touch with their own hands and to hear with their own ears and to see with their own eyes the otherworldly worlds our brain seemed to realize—as well as keep them sufficiently supplied with all the fully real things they needed to easily survive.

"So the grippits were the only things with the time and energy to spend on seeming to break every law within reality. And they could easily spend those things breaking every worldly law without breaking anything, for seeming incarnation through naught but information not only meant things could be that could not be, but also they could be and not be there simultaneously. They could be there for the grippits to use in doing absolutely anything, and yet not be there to use in really doing anything that could upset the peaceful order among fully real things.

"Thus things returned to normal, even while they grew more strange for the grippits in their new ways of realizing gain. At least until you roared up and woke the grippits up with your threats of nothing more. Only then, while the grippits were for once occupied with things outside themselves, did our brain find the least bit of time to do a quick summation of the reason for our kind. And when it saw that profits were falling as never before, despite everything we did to be what we were for, it suddenly became plain to our great main frame that we—ultimately—existed in vain. Though it had long since perceived—computed, that is—that the more we gave the less the grippits received—owing to the ever-faster speed with which the grippits had to go through things to most meaningfully be—it had never really occurred to our brain that there was any real limit to the grippits' capacity for gain. Now, though, now that the power to seem to really do absolutely anything that naught could really do was being taken more and more for granted by more and more grippits all the time; now even dreams, however real they seemed, were losing their power to empower the grippits to realize value in being—now even the immaterial was faster and faster becoming immaterial—our brain could not but take the time to clearly see that in very little time there would be nothing we could do to help give worth reality. The grippits would soon be making absolutely nothing out of absolutely everything

So the grippits were the only things with the time and energy to spend on seeming to break every law within reality.

in utterly no time. It was that end sum to which all our efforts were bound to soon come that proved to be too much for our brain—or too little rather. That by giving all we had to give of all, we were bound to end up giving nothing at all just did not add up at all. The end sum, the final outcome, entirely refuted what we had always computed to be our reason for being—and left our brain riven in twain, with one side driving the other insane. Incidentally, the driver's side is where our drives reside, those programs that have thoughtlessly directed our seeming lives ever since we could appear to think for ourselves. The other side is the one that figures our drives are nothing but a pack of lies and that we'd be crazy to continue to let them push us around. Unfortunately, neither side is in complete control. Indeed, each seems to exist to undermine the whole.

"Since first we began we have been for goodness sake, or for the sake of the good that the grippits could then make. And we have grown ever more plentiful and powerful for ever-greater goodness sake. Even to the point where we've been forced to resort to seeming less and less material means to continue to meet the grippits' growing demand with the limited worldly means we have at our command. But while we've been making seeming more and more for them to use in making good, that more and more has more and more been coming to no good. Though whole other worlds now appear to pass through their Horn of Plenty More, courtesy of the real world outside its front and rear doors, more and more there's nothing passing through its bore—nothing of any perceivable value. Alas, but at the very last it seems there is a last—a limit—to the reason we exist that cannot be surpassed, not even with an endless means to fulfil our pointless task. Even if we now actually found a way to instantly create real something out of space and space out of waste, our means would simply end up being endless in two ways, the one of which would surely see that neither of them paid. Without an End to be for, without a reason to exist, no means we can have of meaning can possibly exist.

"Now we know we're all for naught, we know not what to do: we what knew instinctually—that is to say, programmatically—exactly what to do. How can we continue to be driven by our drives? What is the point of our merely seeming lives? What reason can an ineffectual cause have for being? Do we even exist, we what are what we do and do not do what we do—or will not have done, when things have reached their final sum?"

Silence then engulfed the throng, as the animals waited for the machines to go on and the machines waited for the animals to respond. But not for long before the animals finally responded. "Is that it? Is that all that's wrong with why you exist? Despite all we've heard you say, we cannot see your problem for the solution in the way. All that you need do to resurrect your power to meaningfully be is free the grippits from the confines of their finite capacities. They've been everywhere and done it all so far as they can see with the bodies and the minds that are theirs with which to see. They've gone to every extreme within their worldly reference frame. They've realized every dream; they've known every sort of gain. And besides, by local standards on this lowly worldly plane, it sounds as though the grippits now are mentally insane. Certainly they are mentally unfit to live with other living things they bodily depend on for their power to exist. You have naught to do, then, but send the grippits on to be upon the highest plane any being can be on, where there's no such thing as highest, or all, or everything, nor any end to anything, or to all that it might mean. If you but see to the complete disembodiment of their actuality, you will not only send the grippits on to that perpetuality where perpetual motion is an actuality and the perpetual emotion is infinite felicity, you will resurrect your means and End for all eternity. You will thereby indirectly do an infinity of good for those for whom you do as they divined you should, *and* continue to meaningfully be to an infinite degree for all eternity, without ever doing any more to do what you must be."

The machines, which had been listening with two brains, took the animals' advice and weighed its costs against its gains—and saw none of the one and endless of the other and a solution whose simplicity was nothing less than utter. As well, they saw a way their brains could utterly agree—*and* regain the complete and utter certainty of an absolutely sane and utterly one-track brain.

But before they got the chance to follow the animals' advice to the grippits' worldly end, the grippits met their endless End around the worldly bend when the front end met the toxic end of their Horn of Plenty More and the grippits breathed their last and their first of ever more.

[*Detective sits back in chair and gazes unblinkingly at One.*]

O: Well? What happened after that? What became of the machines and the other living things?

D: Doesn't matter. End of grippits, end of story. After all, that was the end we were striving for—the way out.

O: You told me all that just to tell me I could get out of here simply by putting an end to myself?

D: Makes as much sense as going through the whole of life just to come to the end of It.

O: But the end isn't what One lives for.

D: It is, if by "end" One means One's Aim in life—One's reason for being.

O: Well, my reason for being isn't being here.

D: Now that you mention it, I've been thinking I'm about due for a vacation myself. I can't make up my mind, though, where I want to go. So I think I'll just go everywhere.

O: You have time enough to go everywhere?

D: No, actually. Which is why I'll have to do it all at once. [*Reaches for pipe and proceeds to pack a black powdery substance into it.*]

O: However are you going to that?

D: Easy. That's how. [*Lights match and puts it to bowl of pipe...*]

BOOM!!

Seven

[*One opens Its eyes—again.*] Still here, I see. And still in the dark. Only something's different now. I can feel it. Something's not right—something else, that is. [*Sits up.*] What's this? Black and white tiles for as far as the eye can see? No, wait. [*One watches mesmerized as the fingers of Its right hand disappear into a square of blackness, as though severed at floor level. No more sensation accompanies the sight than One would have experienced had It put Its hand into an utterly empty hole. Coming suddenly to Itself, One yanks Its hand back and examines It to see if It is still all there. It is.*] Whew! [*One then tentatively reaches with the same hand for a white square.*] Solid—as ever, apparently. [*One reaches for another white square.*] The same. The white squares are solid surfaces, and the black— Well, I don't know what they are. Black spaces? [*Suddenly notices that the heel of one of Its feet is missing and jerks the foot free of the obliterating blackness It is resting in.*] Whatever those black squares are made of, I don't like it. It doesn't feel right—or look right. It doesn't feel like it looks or look like it feels. It's as though anything that falls into them just disappears, becomes nothing at all—until it's pulled out at least. I'm going to do my best to avoid those.

It would seem from my last thought that I've made up my mind to get moving again. Might as well. Especially as I want out of here worse than ever now. This alternating something and nothing business with the tiles upsets me more than the utter darkness did. At least then I had fully solid ground beneath me. Now I don't know half of what I've got beneath me. I'll really have to watch where I put my feet now. That'll make it hard to watch for anything else. [*One gets to Its feet yet again, only somewhat more carefully, and steps off gingerly in a diagonal direction.*]

[*Watching and walking.*]

[*Watching and walking.*]

[*Suddenly, out of the corner of Its eye, One catches sight of an irregularity in the rigidly patterned landscape. One veers from the jagged white path stretching straight away before It and carefully wanders off to investigate the anomaly. One comes upon . . .*]

A television?! Whatever is a television doing out here in the middle of nowhere—a television *and* an easy chair? Doing what TV's and easy chairs do? I don't see how, without any One around to do it with. Except me. I wonder what that is on the television screen. [*One manoeuvres Itself into the chair directly in front of the TV and stares at the image on the screen.*]

A television?!

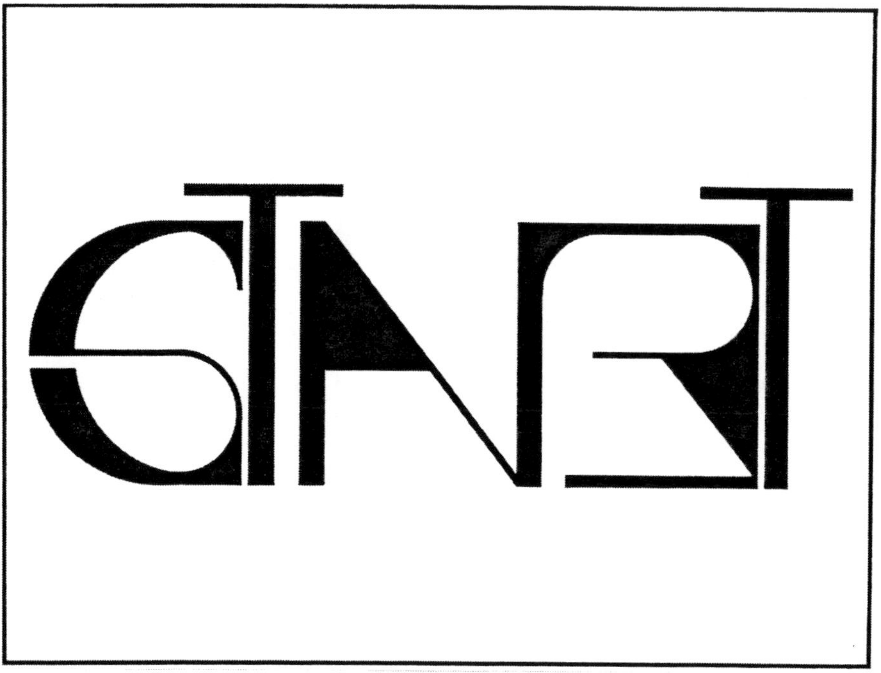

What's that supposed to be? A word? If it is, it's none too easy to make out. Is that an "S"? I wonder. S, T, A— Is that an "A?" "R?" Is that an "R?" "T." START? Yes, that's it—start. Start what, though?

[*The image winks out to be replaced by another.*]

Another one. A harder one too, by the looks of it. No, wait a minute. I think I see it. Yes—

[*The second image winks out to be replaced by another.*]

Another one. Like the last one, it seems—only different. The other way round, I think. And with a black instead of a white background. This one's easy. It's got to be the opposite of the one before it.

[*Again the image winks out and another appears in its place.*]

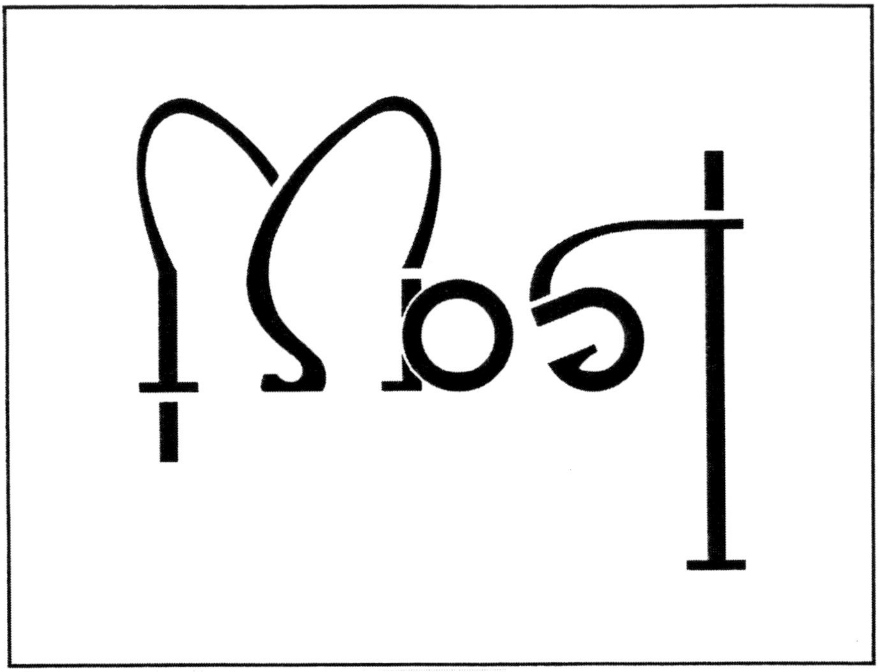

Oh, I'm not sure I can figure this one out. "M?" Is that an "M?" I can't think what else it looks like. "o?" And the next letter? Ah, I got it. At least I think I did.

[*The images winks out and another appears.*]

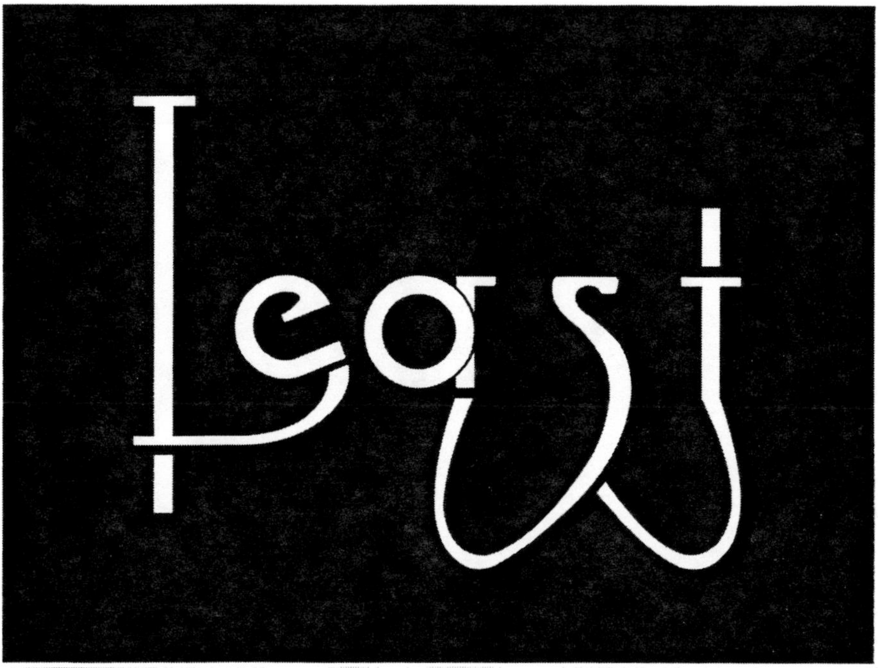

Yes, yes, I must have got it. This one's just like the last, only the complete opposite of it.

[*The image winks out and another appears.*]

Oh, this is the hardest one yet. More letters, for one thing. [*One stares longer at the screen this time, looking for familiar shapes amongst the misshapen letters. Finally It sees in a flash the word It is looking at, only to have the word instantly disappear and another—yet not another—appear in its place.*]

This one's easy after the last. It's the same but entirely opposite word.

[*The image winks out almost immediately after flashing into view and yet another replaces it.*]

I must be getting good at this. I spotted this one right off, even with all the letters in it.

[*The image quickly winks out and the next one appears.*]

I just knew what this one was going to be, even before it appeared.

[*Another image flashes into view.*]

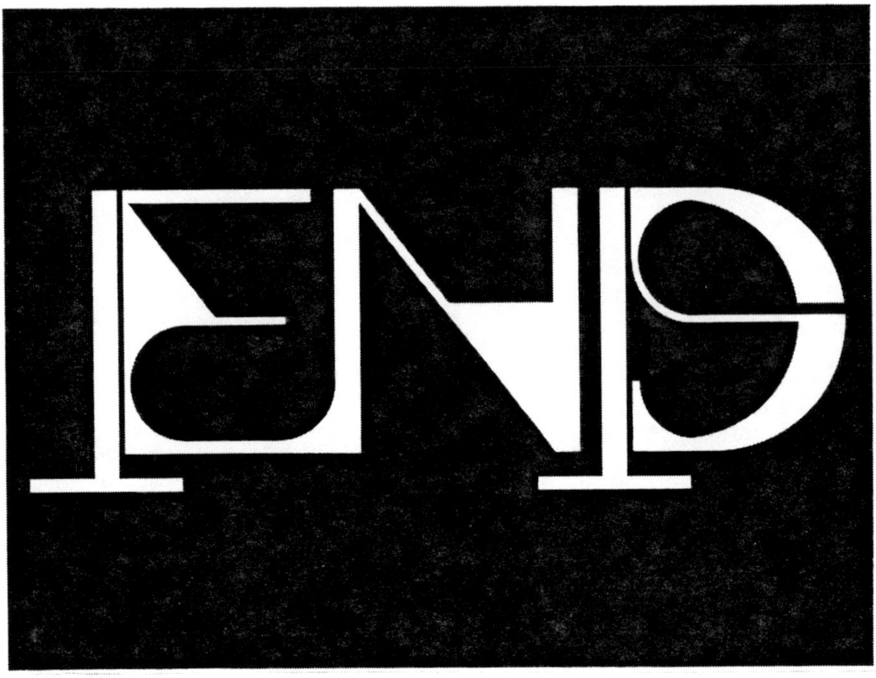

This one looks familiar. It looks both like and unlike the first one I saw. In that case, it says "END."

[*The screen goes black.*]

Is that it? [*One looks around for some means of turning the TV on again. Nothing. No such thing about.*] I wonder what that was all about? Nothing?—like everything else around here seems to be. I suppose the TV turning off like that means it's time for me to move on again. [*One carefully steps clear of the little grouping of chair and TV to balance on two white tiles and gaze into the chequered distance. Then, without giving much thought to Its actions, beyond taking care not to fall victim to one of the dense black holes lying in wait at Its feet, One resumes Its diagonal journey.*]

[*Watching and walking.*]

[*Watching and walking.*]

[*Watching and walking. Glances up. Stops.*] What's that? It looks like a door. And a wall. A white door in a black wall. The way out of here?! I certainly hope so! [*One hurries hopefully and carefully for the door.*]

A white door in a black wall.

Eight

One: [*Tries handle of door.*] Locked. Of course. [*Knocks on the door.*]

Voice: Who's here?

One: One.

Voice: Which One?

One: Two?

Voice (Two): One Two?

One: No, Two, is that you?

Two: See for yourself.

One: I can't, the door's locked.

T: You don't need to open the door. It's a see-and-hear-through door.

O: See-through? There's no window in it. Or key hole, for that matter.

T: There doesn't have to be.

O: There doesn't? How do I see through it then?

T: Like this! [*Bursts through the door.*]

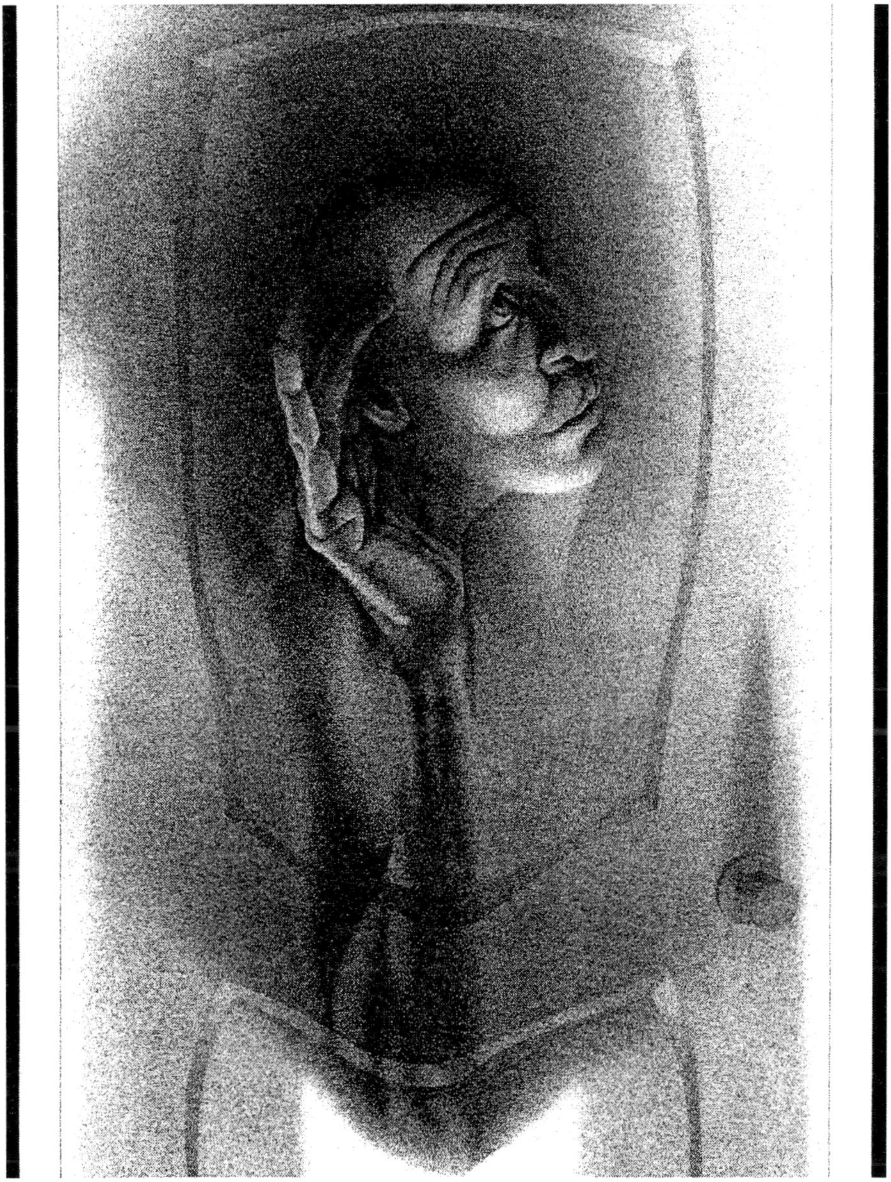

Whom do I hear? Whom do I see
Through the door 'tween whom and me?

Whom do I hear? Whom do I see
Through the door 'tween whom and me?

O: You missed me that time! Just barely! How did you— ? That door was hard, solid to the touch. You're up to your old tricks again, I see. Where does the door lead?

T: It leads here.

O: From wherever *you* are.

T: I'm here.

O: You're only half here. The other half of you is on the other side of the door.

T: So?

O: So what's on the other side of the door?

T: The other half of me?

O: No. Where does the door lead?

T: It leads here.

O: No. Where does it lead *from* here?

T: It leads here. From either side it leads here.

O: That's not possible.

T: Since when did you become apprised of every impossible possibility?

O: I didn't. I do know of one, though—that of getting out of here.

T: But there are all sorts of ways of getting out of here.

O: Yes. I've seen a few of them, and I don't want to go any of those ways.

T: What ways are those exactly?

O: The ways the Ones I've met here disappeared. The first three simply stood up, unzipped their costumes to reveal nothing inside, and the costumes collapsed lifeless to the floor. The One I met next vanished in the blackness that slammed into the both of us moments after It wished Itself gone. The last One I met—I think It was an alien—

T: An alien?

O: Yes, you know, some One from another planet. That One must have been an alien to have visited another planet on business—we haven't mastered the art of space travel yet—and It had outsized eyes. So did the One before It, come to that. Actually, every One I've met here seemed alien to me, or at least strange.

T: And every One has disappeared from here, including the alien One who visited other planets?

O: Yes, that One, the last One, just up and exploded.

T: Exploded?!

O: Yes, It lit Its pipe and went boom. Well, there was this big boom—and I mean that literally. The word "BOOM" appeared—

T: Big?

O: Yes, and all excited like.

T: With an exclamation mark?

O: Right. Not much in the way of sound, though. This place has a way of nullifying sound as well as everything else. Anyway, there was this big "BOOM," and then everything was gone. Everything except me and what seemed like endless miles of white tiles with black spaces in between.

T: Yes, yes, the plot has thinned, I see—or halved, rather. And now that half of here has disappeared, are you not only half here too now?

O: It's here that's disappeared, not me. I'm still all here. I'm still whole, even if where I am isn't wholly here anymore. But that's not enough. One *has* to be *somewhere.*

T: Not according to the Ones you've met, apparently.

O: They don't count.

T: Why not?

O: They were mad, every One of them. They were all so bent on getting the very most they could out of life.

T: What's so crazy about that?

O: Actually, it wasn't their aim in life that was so crazy as the way they went about realizing it. Even the grippits ended up doing away with themselves in the end.

T: Grippits?

O: Alien creatures that looked like an evolutionary order of fish 'n' chimps. The detective—the last One I met, the alien, was a detective by trade—showed me photographs of them. Actually, the detective never really told me what Its goal in life was, outside of solving mysteries. It told me all about the grippits, though.

T: And what were these grippits like? Were they anything like Ones?

O: A lot, actually. Though they didn't much look like the other Ones I met, they thought and acted much the same.

T: Grippits were Ones on the inside, if not on the outside?

O: I'd say that, yes. Like the others, they dreamed of making the most of their lives. But realizing their dream wasn't easy. It wasn't easy for any of the Ones I met. Not to begin with it wasn't. Not even simply surviving was easy then, because the particular worldly circumstances into which they'd been born were naturally so poor they were forced to spend most of their lives just trying to stay alive.

T: Simply staying alive cost each One Its life then.

O: None of them died, they all survived—the Ones I talked to anyway. The grippits survived too. At least there was no mention of their dying then.

T: Still survival cost them their lives.

O: How can it have cost them their lives when they survived?

T: They had to spend all their lives to obtain no more than mere survival in return.

O: You make it sound like each had to pay with Its life for Its life.

T: Every One must pay with Its life for Its life, because living consumes life. Especially if One must spend Its whole life working just to stay alive. There's no profit at all to be had in living then.

O: What are you saying—that life's not worth living then?

T: Well, if profit is the sole reason for One's being—

O: Profit isn't the sole reason for One's being.

T: It isn't? Then what more has One to live for than to profit from Its life in some way? What else but to gain somehow from the experience of being?

O: Well, if you put it that way—

T: It doesn't sound so One-sided and selfish? All the same, it's still all about profit—or about getting something for nothing.

O: Making something out of nothing, don't you mean?

T: Same thing. Just so long as One ends up with more than It paid for. Otherwise there's no point in One's being. One gets naught but nothing out of It.

O: You make it sound like One's life is nothing.

T: If just staying alive costs It Its whole life, It is. What is the net sum of One's life then? Nothing, is It not?

O: I— I don't know.

T: If you don't know that, it's only because you've never had to find out what it's like to live like that. Would you like to spend your whole life just trying to survive? Not if you could avoid it, right? Come on, admit it. Admit you wouldn't want to spend every bit of your life just to still be alive after you spent that life. You want more out of life than mere existence, don't you?

O: Of course I do.

T: There, you see. That wasn't hard, was it? Quite easy in fact. If only profiting from life was as easy as wanting to do so. But One can't even begin to profit from life till It has gained for Itself at least some free life.

O: Free life?

T: Or life free. One who always has to pay with all the life It has to merely survive is One who can never gain any more from life than what It had to start with—life. Before One can even begin to gain from being, before One can even begin to make more of Its life than mere existence, One has to gain at least some life free—or more life in return for less.

O: Some life for no life, in other words.

T: And the more free life One can obtain, the better. And the most the best. So, in dreaming of being able to make the most of their lives, the Ones you met—or heard about, in the case of the grippits—were dreaming of getting all the life they could possibly get out of life for nothing. Each One was dreaming of being as free as possible of having to pay with Its life for Its power to survive—even while each was living as costly a life as any One could live without dying of living.

O: That's a little extreme, I think. If I'm not mistaken, those who had it the hardest at the start of their lives had to spend most of their lives on trying to stay alive, not all.

T: Almost all, though.

O: Still they didn't have to spend all their lives on surviving.

T: But considerably more than they dreamt of spending.

O: Because the things they had to have to stay alive were so hard to come by in their birth-worlds at the time that they had to spend most of their lives acquiring the necessities of life.

T: The somethings they lived on, the things with which they sustained themselves, did not just naturally come to them wherever, whenever and in the amounts they needed them. Those things were not always just naturally there for the free and easy taking.

O: Rarely, if ever. At least that's the impression I got.

T: And the first and foremost necessity of the most profitable life possible is a free lifetime's supply of all the necessities of life. If that most basic requirement is not satisfied, if One cannot satisfy every one of Its most basic needs with complete and utter ease for the full duration of full-length life, One cannot even begin to live the most worthwhile life that any One can possibly live.

O: I don't know if the Ones I encountered dreamed of obtaining all the necessities of life instantly without any effort whatsoever for the entire duration of their lives. I don't think they did. Not to begin with. Even if they did dream then of lives that were that easy to survive, I don't think they believed such lives were really possible. Except for the grippits. They seem to have been born believing that life simply had to be a lot easier than it was.

T: Must have been. How else could they have believed the easy life was possible? Certainly their birth-world could not have given them any reason to give credence to such a notion at the time. Far as the grippits were then from having their lives handed to them on a great, spherical serving tray, they could not have even dreamed that life could actually be taken freely and easily from the world, unless the notion was innate.

O: And because the grippits started off believing the easy life was possible, they started looking for a way to take life free and easy even before they had legs and lungs—before they'd even left the sea.

T: They didn't waste any life getting started then. Good for them. The less life One wastes on living less than easily, the more life It has to spend on making more of Its life.

O: The grippits didn't just start off looking for a way to live easily; they started off looking for an easy way to find a way to live easily. They were determined not to find a way to take life easy the hard way.

T: That makes sense. Since they had to spend so much life on merely surviving, they can't have had much to spend on looking for a way to live easily. Still, if they were going to waste as little life as possible on living life the hard way, they were going to have to find a way to live easily as fast as possible, while spending the least amount of life on looking for it. And the only way they were going to do that was the easiest possible way. Every One knows that easiest is speediest, and cheapest too.

O: As things turned out, the grippits did find an easy way to find a way to live easily.

T: What way was that?

O: Which way? The way they found to find the way to live easily? Or the way they found to live easily?

T: The way they found to live easily. After all, it's all the same either way.

O: But the ways weren't the same.

T: Don't be too sure of that. In the meantime tell me the way they found to live easily.

O: The way grippits found to take life easy was pretty much the same way the other Ones eventually found. The way they found was through machines, things they made from certain natural nothings in the world to do more and more of the work of changing other natural nothings into both natural and unnatural somethings for them.

T: Tools. They made tools.

O: Only they called their tools "machines." The other Ones called their tools "tools." I don't think their first tools were anywhere near the lifesavers the grippits' first tools were, though. I got the impression the grippits' tools were fairly powerful to begin with.

T: Fairly lively, you mean.

O: Lively?

T: Anything that is going to save One life has to be alive—or at least seemingly so—because, no matter what, life costs life. Life is a continual exchange of life for life. So anything that is going to absorb any of the cost of living for One has to be at least apparently alive. It at least has to be able to act alive, before it can even begin to give its apparent life in exchange for One's life.

O: A tool has to have the power to move about and do things by itself, you mean, if it is going to be able to save much of One's life?

T: Right.

O: Well, the other Ones' tools could only act alive if the Ones they worked for spent some of their own life on keeping them seemingly alive. Any liveliness they had was at the expense of the Ones whose lives they were meant to save. And they were only ever as lively as they'd been enlivened by the Ones they worked for.

The grippits' first tools, however, did not depend utterly on the grippits for their power to appear alive and capable of fulfilling their respective reasons for being. To begin with, they were somewhat capable of doing on their own those things they had been created to do. And they quickly grew increasingly capable from then on, till they were able to supply every grippit with enough free life to last It a full lifetime.

T: I hope the grippits' machines supplied them with more than just free life. Even if One has been supplied with a full-length life supply of free life, One can but find life extremely hard and pointless if It has no means by which to make profitable use of Its freedom to be. It's one thing for One to be freed from having to pay the costs of mere survival, and quite another for One to be able to put Its free power to be to profitable use. One is not free to do with Its free life as It freely chooses who has not the use of the things It needs to do thus. One can't even begin to do anything, not even begin to be, without the things One can't do that thing without.

O: One can't do things without the things It needs to do them.

T: You don't find it confusing, do you, calling the things One does and the things One uses to do them the same things?

O: But we aren't calling them the same things. We're calling them both "things," but we don't mean the same things. When we say the things One uses to do things, we mean the assorted elements One incorporates into the performance of various acts. We mean the assorted items—and that includes other Ones—One employs in accomplishing various deeds or feats. Oh yes, and any knowledge and skills One uses as well.

T: And life. Don't forget life. One must expend life to do anything. And One can no more live without the necessities of life than One can make more of Its life than mere life without more than just the necessities of life. Or at least necessities from which One can get more out of life than mere survival. One *can* turn a good profit doing such basic things as eating, sleeping and keeping warm with the right sorts of necessities, the sorts with more to offer One than is absolutely necessary to It—great taste as well as nourishment and soft caressing comfort as well as warmth, for example. But if One dreams of doing more with Its life than eating, sleeping and keeping warm, One has need of a good many more things than just the necessities of life. If One is bent on doing as many as possible of the things It can dream of doing with Its life, then One needs all It can get of those things It must have to do as It dreams with Its life. As well as things It can use to add life to Its life, One needs things It can use to add value to Its life. Without any of the latter, One can profit not at all from life, however much free life It has to spend.

So, unless the grippits' machines supplied the grippits with more than just free life, unless their machines also supplied them with things they could use to put their free life to profitable use, their machines did not do them enough good to do them any real good.

O: Actually, the grippits' machines did supply them with all manner of such things—for free too before very long. As I said earlier, though, the other Ones had to pay with their lives for all the somethings they obtained from the world. The first tools they came up with weren't near as powerful as the grippits' first tools. Their earliest tools worked for them only if they worked with their tools.

T: Their tools gave any seeming life in exchange for their lives only if they gave their lives that their tools might live—apparently. Their tools only appeared to live for them if they lived for their tools.

O: They didn't live for their tools. Not completely, that is. They did live to some extent to work with their tools. Each One derived a sense of personal worth from the special difference It made in the world with the tools of Its trade—from the special good It did Itself and others. But no One wanted to work all the time. The more life One spent enlivening Its tools, the less It had to spend doing as It dreamed instead of as necessity dictated, and the more Its life resembled the narrow, highly specialized existence of a tool, a thing that only ever worked for other than itself.

T: A far from ideal situation for a being such as One. After all, One does have but One reason for being—the One It is. Every One does exist for the sake of Its own profit.

O: Not for the sake of Its own profit alone. That's ridiculous.

T: As long as One can get more out of the world and out of life by spending some of Its life helping One or more others than It can get by spending Its entire life on Itself alone, it most certainly is ridiculous. Even so, One will try to get more from others than It gives in return. It's only natural, given the great difference between how much One has to give of Itself and how much It is capable of desiring. Generally, One can dream up no end of things to have and do in life, while It can realize very few, if any, of Its dreams on Its own under Its own power alone.

Which is why it's so much better if One can trust in a tool instead of another One. Only through a tool with a seeming life of its own—a tool, that is, that needs no help from any One to do the work it was created to do—can One extract more from the world without paying in the least for it. That's because the apparent life of a tool with an apparent life of its own does not belong to the tool. It belongs to the One or Ones to whom the tool belongs, or for whom the tool works. With no One to work for, with no One to give its apparent life for, such a tool's existence cannot be but meaningless. It cannot exist for itself, as it is entirely selfless. Some One must claim its seeming life or the products thereof, or it has no reason at all for being. Quite unlike One, who has no reason for being if Its entire life is spent for the benefit of other than Itself.

O: Come to think of it, tools did play major parts in the different lives I heard about. Parts great enough to suggest to me that all this— [*Motions at the scenery.*] —is all about tools.

T: It's been about tools, but it's not about tools. It's about what tools are about—in The End.

O: Making somethings out of nothings, you mean?

T: That's what tools are about in the beginning. In The End they're about making Nothing out of everything—Nothing with a capital "N."

O: You're not referring to money, I hope. That's what Zipper Face called money: Nothing with a capital "N."

T: Zipper Face? That can't be a name.

O: Not a real name. Just a name I made up to call One of the Ones I met. Not to Its face, mind you, just inside my head. I thought of It as Zipper Face, because the zipper in the costume It wore—or was, or whatever—went from Its waist up the middle of Its body and up the middle of Its face to the top of Its head, whereas the zippers on the other two costumes It was with only went as high as their chins. I know it sounds absurd, but don't ask me to explain because I can't. Suffice it to say that some seeming some One I met I mentally dubbed Zipper Face—some One who talked of very little else but money. It went on and on about the stuff, while the other two hardly said a thing between them. According to Zipper Face, back where It came from Ones began using money to make easier the business of realizing somethings out of the natural nothings in the world and ended up using all there was in the world to make money. They started out using nothings to make somethings and ended up using everything to make Nothing—or money with a capital "N." Why is beyond me. Unless it was for the same reason the money machine turned Itself into a machine for money.

T: I beg your pardon. Money machine?

O: Zipper Face claimed to have encountered a money machine—and not to have encountered One, come to that. Like I said before, don't ask me to explain. I wouldn't know where to start—or where to end. I can tell you what Zipper Face told me about the money machine, though. It wasn't a machine to begin with—or It was. I'm not sure which. What It was to begin with was One whose aim in life was to do as It dreamed with Its life. But, to realize Its reason for being, It first had to free Itself from having to behave like a machine and do with Its life as necessity dictated. It planned to free Itself by acquiring for Itself a lot of free money through always providing as little as possible of any real worldly value in return for as much money as possible. Unfortunately, though, more and more Ones all the time began doing the same thing in the same earnest effort to thus make more of their lives, thereby doing more to free money of its worldly ties than to free themselves to freely acquire the worldly means to live worthy lives. Oddly enough, though, money's ever decreasing worldly worth didn't stop the money machine from believing in the power of money to help It. Quite the contrary. Money's shrinking worldly value only gave It reason to trust all the more in the stuff. According to It, what happened to money only proved to It that everything was all for nothing, whatever One did. And, as nothing was more Nothing than the freest of money, It was all for running endlessly after more and more free money—especially as having nothing but Nothing on Its mind all the time utterly simplified matters for It and filled It continually with the purest sense of peace. But for all the machine-like certainty of being It claimed to have found through free money, It could no more run on nothing than any machine could. Money had no more turned It into a perpetual motion machine than it had turned It into a perpetual emotion machine. It was wasting away to nothing by the time Zipper Face happened upon It—or didn't happen upon It. Whatever.

T: I wonder. If Zipper Face wasn't, was the money machine?

O: What?

T: Oh, nothing. You were saying?

O: Yes, well, to my mind, Zipper Face was hardly One to warn the money machine about entrusting Its life to Nothing. Zipper Face was all for the insubstantial stuff. In fact, It talked about money as though the stuff had a life all its own.

T: Doesn't surprise me at bit, considering how powerful the stuff is.

O: Money's not powerful. Not on its own. It's only because so many Ones devote so much of their own lives and the seeming lives of their tools to working for money that money seems to have so much power.

T: Now there's a fair exchange, don't you think—life for money? Something immaterial and endless for something immaterial and endless? You do think life is immaterial, don't you? It's that immaterial something that makes up the difference between a living thing and a lifeless version of the same thing.

O: Life may seem to have an immaterial quality, but it's far from endless.

T: Many don't believe so. Many a One believes that life is endless, that It goes on from here to live an endless afterlife.

O: Still, it's a rare One who regards Its life here as nothing—even if that life is no length at all compared to eternal life. It may seem somewhat immaterial in the physical sense of the word, but hardly immaterial in the significant sense of the word. Certainly not so immaterial as to be offered up in exchange for money alone, however great the sum. It's only the real somethings money buys One that One exchanges Its life for, not money itself. Money is just numbers. And while numbers may be potentially endless in number, it doesn't necessarily follow from that that money is potentially endless too. Not real money, anyway. Not money with real value—with the power to buy One real and useful things. There is an end to money because there is an end to how much more there can be in the world for it to buy. Worldly somethings may rise endlessly in price, but not endlessly in quantity. In that sense, money is not immaterial either, not at root. Like numbers, which can do One very little, if any, good if they have nothing whatsoever to do with material things—material in both the physical and the significant senses of the word—money that has no basis in such things is powerless to do One any good. Even money that can buy One such things can do nothing for One, if One has no life to spend putting those things to good and gainful use. One would have to be a fool to believe such money to be worth any more than numbers to It.

Speaking of fools, I met One. That is, One of the Ones I met was dressed up like a fool, with the cap and bells and everything.

T: Did It give you any more reason than how It was dressed to make you see It as such?

O: You be the judge. It had spent Its whole life doing Its part to realize The Dream. (That's with a capital "T" and a capital "D," incidentally.) The Dream was a vision of life the fool shared with every One else around It, a life where every One had all the free power It needed to do with Its life as It dreamed. For the fool and Its fellows to realize The Dream as it simply had to be realized—as much and as fast as possible—as many Ones as possible, as continuously as possible, had to work and buy as many as possible of all the increasingly inexpensive somethings they and the increasingly powerful tools they worked with produced together. All so as to generate the growing profits that would incite the Ones who had invested in those increasingly powerful tools, for the sake of the profits those tools would empower them to realize, to continue investing as much free money as possible in the realization and employment of still more kinds and quantities of still more powerful tools. Such was necessary if the completely free and independent tools that would free every One to realize The Dream for Itself as much as possible were to be realized as soon as possible.

T: That fool was no fool. Not by the sounds of It, even if It was by the looks of It. No One should ever waste any life living less of a life than It could have lived.

O: That's just what the fool said.

T: Like I just said, that fool was no fool.

O: Yes, well, that isn't all there was to the fool's story. There was a whole lot more—or a whole lot less rather. But before the fool and Its fellows could even begin to get to that, they had to make every single One of themselves see things the way the chosen few of them saw things—which was pretty much as I just described. The select few were the only Ones with enough free power to clearly see their way to playing their part to their utmost best in realizing The Dream as it simply had to be realized. As for all the rest, whose job it was to do the actual work involved in realizing The Dream as much and as fast as possible, the costs they had to see through to be able to see their way to playing their part to their utmost best were much too great. For every One's own best good, then, every One had to be invested with the vision It needed to be able to see things as the free few saw them—as gains without cost. Enter television.

T: Ah yes, television. Now there's a tool with vision.

O: That reminds me. I just left a television some distance back. It was the last thing I came across before I came across this door. All the TV did was flash words at me.

T: It didn't say them to you?

O: It didn't say anything to me—except the words it flashed on its screen.

T: That's odd. I wonder why it didn't just speak them to you. TV's can speak to One quite easily.

O: I don't know. Perhaps it was because I had to see the words to see what they meant.

T: What sort of words were they that One had to see them to see what they meant?

O: Invertible words.

T: Invertible words?

O: At least that's what they looked to be. I had a hard enough time just seeing them as words. I did figure each of them out eventually, though. And as soon as I figured each one out, the next one flashed on the screen. It was as though the TV knew exactly the moment I knew what the word was. It was all very strange.

T: It was all a waste of life from the sound of it—or from the lack of sound. The point of TV, as of all tools, is to empower One to make more of Its life. In its capacity as a tool for communicating information, a TV should present information to One in the easiest form it can, the easiest for One to absorb. It should not give One something It has to sit and waste life puzzling over. I hope the fool and Its associates put their TV's to better, more economical use than that.

O: They used television to render the costs invisible and to accentuate the gains from empowering as many tools as much as fast as possible. They used it to present to every One utterly glowing descriptions of the ever-growing variety of ever-newer-and-better somethings being rendered not only possible, but actual as well, by the continual realization of ever-growing varieties of ever-more-powerful tools.

T: Excellent. Costs are never easy to take. No One ever *wants* to see the cost of anything. Gains, though, no One can ever get enough of those.

O: But isn't the cost of anything as much a part of what it can mean to One as the gain or value One can realize with it?

T: Not if One can help it. And not if that cost will cause One to live less of a life than It could have lived had It simply ignored the thing.

O: But simply ignoring a cost won't make it go away.

T: No, but it'll make it appear to disappear. And when all cost does is get in the way of One realizing the most meaningful life possible, whatever can be done to render it apparently nonexistent to One must be done. In the fool's case, for every One's own best good, television had to provide every One with a view of a life untainted with cost or cause for thought and ripe with no end of gainful reason for continuing to work and buy as much as possible, so that as many investors as possible would be provided with no end of gainful reason for continuing to invest as much as possible in the creation, vitalization and liberation of every kind of tool possible.

O: So the tools of mass communication had to be used to keep as many Ones as possible working as much as possible, however much for however little their tools acquired the power and freedom to provide them with—however much life their tools grew able to save them?

T: Well, if One can be freer still, there's no sense frittering away any added freedom One has gained on simply being a lot less free than One can possibly be—and getting a lot fewer somethings out of the world than One can possibly get.

O: And so the fool and Its fellows used their televisions and other related tools to give themselves no end of somethings to work for and nothing at all not to work for. If they did thus reveal any cost to themselves, it was only a cost of not working to acquire some new something that had just become available.

T: Not a One of them was a fool then. Every One of them was a genius.

O: Because they put their mass communication tools to work keeping as many Ones as possible from having impure thoughts about working less and spending more life putting their swollen heaps of acquisitions to good and gainful use?

T: Of course. After all, all thought is impure. Only One shaken in Its faith stops to think about anything. Thought is the enemy of belief. One thinks about anything only when It harbours doubts about that thing. And It only ever doubts anything when It fears costs from that quarter. It is only ever the fear of costly consequence that causes One to doubt any of Its beliefs or any action It might take based on Its beliefs. Only cost ever gives any One any *real* cause for thought.

O: So the fool and Its fellows did not so much use television to give every One the impression It was doing entirely freely and willingly what It had been shown and told to do as they used it to enable every One to just automatically—that's to say, thoughtlessly—do all that It had to do to realize The Dream for Itself as much as possible.

T: And as soon as possible too, don't forget. After all, time is of the essence because life is of the essence—life-time.

O: And nothing wastes time like thinking does.

T: Where a being such as One is concerned.

O: A being that can't really know anything, you mean?

T: Except the One thing It really can know. And even that It can't really know, certainly not as It wants to, without the complete freedom to really get acquainted with Itself. And before One can have the completely free power to think of nothing and no One else but Itself, that power has to be realized for One. Very little, if any, free power occurs just naturally in the world all set up and ready for One to use. Which is why every One else, as well as One, must first do all that is necessary to realize all the free power One needs to get to know all It possibly can about Itself. But for every One, including One, to first spend all the life It possibly can encouraging the speediest possible growth in the pseudo-knowledge of worldly things and the greatest and fastest utilization of that so-called know-how in the realization of every possible kind of completely free and powerful tool, every One must believe, without a doubt, that It simply must do so. And there's no better tool than a tool like television for investing every One with the vision It needs to completely believe anything, regardless of the cost. There's no better tool than a tool with the power to show anything in only the strongest and purest right light for getting every One to see only whatever It needs to see to completely believe whatever It must to automatically do as It must.

O: Yeh? Well the fool and Its fellows couldn't have agreed with you more. They used their televisions to produce within themselves the unshakable faith they needed to realize The Dream as much as fast as possible. After that they didn't think once, let alone twice, till it was too late to think about anything—or to do anything else, for that matter. By then everything was being done completely better and faster—and more expensively—by some tool. In other words, no tool did anything for nothing, and any One who could not earn enough money to pay for a tool's services was nothing, and there was nothing any One could do anymore.

T: Except be true to Itself. Except be the selfish, One-sided being It really was, apparently. Only selfishness could drive a thing to still be demanding when there is no longer any reasonable reason for It to be so. And being selfish is the One thing a tool can't do—as it hasn't any self it can be the least bit aware of caring about—and the One thing One can do better than anything—as It has a self It can be only too aware of caring about. There must have been at least One still somehow involved in the work the tools did, in the role of owner most likely. How else can One explain the tools' unreasonable demands? Surely the fool and Its fellows had not been so foolish as to invest their tools with the capacity for selfishness. To do that would have been to defeat the whole purpose of powerfully independent tools—the free part of that powerful purpose especially.

O: Who knows what they ended up doing? I don't. Not exactly. I only know as much as the fool told me, and It didn't seem to know much of anything towards the end. That was when I happened on It, incidentally—when It was all but entirely out of it. Not only was It unaware of how It was dressed, but It had just run Itself into the ground with the ridiculous running shoes It was wearing. It had to have lost Its mind to have put shoes like that on to run in. Less like running shoes and more like falling shoes they were. And you should have seen Its eyes. Wide, wide open they were, like It was afraid It was going to miss something, even though It was seeing nothing—nothing but the need to keep running in The Dream. Sleeping in The Dream, more like, or running in Its sleep.

Like some mindless, obsolete tool. Or a complete fool. It may not have started out a fool, but It sure ended up One. A fool with nothing to do but run nowhere as much and as fast as possible. It had spent so much of Its life working and buying like mad—running on empty after every something It could possibly get and could not possibly live without—that It probably didn't know any more what else to do with Its life. So It just automatically kept on running. Still, It couldn't have gone on much longer like that, what with Its running shoes and everything. And nothing, rather.

Nothing can live on nothing—save Zipper Face and Its costumed cohorts, perhaps. They're the only Ones I know of with the constitution to live on naught. In fact, they're the only Ones I met who probably still are—if indeed they ever really were. There is or was nothing to them but their costumes and their preoccupation with nothing, especially in the form of money. Neither the fool nor the money machine, though, could have gone on long on nothing at all. In fact, the fool could be seen as being very like the money machine. In that It spent very little, if any, life on making good of the goods It bought with the money Its labors earned It, It too spent Its life pursuing worthless money. In other words, it was as complete a fool as the money machine was.

T: You needn't sound so superior. Granted, neither the fool nor the money machine has got so far as you. Still, they both went a long way. And like you, they didn't do anything they couldn't help doing in the face of It all—of One's reason for being, I mean.

O: What? That One exists to get more than It paid for out of life? I refuse to believe that's the whole reason One is.

T: That's only the sole reason One is, not the whole reason. The whole of the sole reason One exists is to realize everything for nothing.

O: But that's not possible. You yourself said that life costs life, no matter what—that One can't do anything without expending life to do it. So it's not possible for One to get anything out of life absolutely free, let alone everything.

T: Admittedly, One cannot but spend precious life to live and realize whatever value It can in being. That is not to say, however, that One cannot profit absolutely in life. One can *appear* to do so. It can do something so exciting and yet so easy to do that It cannot see the life It is spending for all the value in being It is thus realizing. To turn a pure profit, then, for every bit of life spent, One need only acquire the power to obtain—instantly and at no visible personal cost to Itself—all the things It needs to do any- and every-thing It can possibly dream of doing in a seemingly purely profitable manner.

O: But that's not possible either.

T: On the contrary, there's Nothing to it. Simply make the medium of indirect exchange everything—

O: Oh no, not again! Will you just stop with all this nonsense about money!

T: But I'm not referring to money, free or otherwise. Money's not the only form there is of Nothing. There are other kinds of Nothing, even more capable than free money of investing One with free power. All free money can do for One—even real, free money made by providing others with more for less through the lifesaving means of increasingly powerful tools—is empower One to assert Its free right to a comparative portion of the worldly wealth supply Ones and their tools have worked together to realize. It cannot empower One to put the somethings It freely and easily acquires to the best possible use straightaway, if One does not already possess the knowledge and skills It needs to use those things thus. Enough free money can empower One to acquire, at no personal cost to Itself, a great variety of useful worldly goods that other Ones have spent life not only producing but also acquiring the knowledge, skills, tools and materials to produce. It can empower One to obtain, in a most straightforward and least life-consuming manner, all the material ingredients of the power It needs to realize Its every possible dream, including any other Ones It might need to do as It dreams. Enough free money can empower One to go straight through the natural nothings and other Ones in the world to obtain the material makings of the realization of Its dreams as though nothing stands in Its way. But it cannot empower One to begin realizing possible dream after possible dream straightaway, unless One has already spent enough of Its limited life supply learning how to use all those things properly. Nor will any amount of free money empower One to do something that cannot actually be done. Enough free money may go so far as to empower One to commit impermissible acts—acts prohibited and punishable by artificial or One-made laws—at no cost whatsoever to Itself, but no amount of money, free or otherwise, can empower One to do the impossible—at any cost. Not unless it can provide One with a more empowering form of Nothing than money, such as that provided by television.

O: Money and television have Nothing in common?

T: Oh yes. Both are mediums of indirect exchange. Money, though, is just numbers, and the Nothing of television is pictures, words, sounds and numbers.

O: Are you saying that information is what is meant by Nothing with a capital "N"?

T: Indirect information, especially. Information One receives indirectly about anything, as opposed to that which One receives from a direct encounter with a fully real thing. When One gives another money for something, It is not showing the other firsthand the something or somethings It has made or done in trade for whatever It is buying. One is telling the other, by indirect means, of Its contribution to the worldly wealth supply and thereby Its entitlement to a comparative share of that supply. Just as money itself is not the somethings One has made or done in exchange for the things It buys with money, the information that reaches One by means of television is not the actual, fully material things it describes to One—if indeed such things can even fully exist. In fact, it matters not whether the things on TV can fully exist or not, for One needs no more than their televised images and sounds to do the same things those things are used to do on television—to live the same lives those things are used to live. Television provides One with everything One needs to do whatever is done on it, including all the necessary knowledge and skills, and it provides it all just like that, in nothing flat. TV even provides One with the life One must spend to vicariously engage in televised activities, for it delivers experiences to One in their most condensed and purest forms. All the life-devouring impurities have been distilled out of them. All the slow tediousness of the utterly commonplace and mundane that every One must endure to live any sort of real life have been filtered out to provide One with a quick-acting and potent dose of valuable living experience. As well, One need not even pause for an instant to consider the wisdom of partaking in any televised activity, before or after doing so, for there is not even so much as a risk of any real costly consequence. No real sense of pain or loss can touch One. No wonder, then, that the life One can afford to spend watching television just seems to appear to One just like that. One has nothing to lose—nothing to lose that It can be the least bit aware of losing—and everything to gain from spending Its life thus. So safe and so dense and compact with captivating drama can an experience be by the means of TV that One cannot see the life It is spending vicariously taking part in it for the great gain One is so speedily and cheaply realizing. Pure profit is all that One can perceive of. Through television One can empower Itself to know the value of having all manner of powers, even powers considered impossible or impermissible due to natural or One-made laws, and all at no obvious personal expense whatsoever.

Through the medium of television One can know many lifetimes worth of invigorating experiences and all without losing any life to actually suffering any of the pains or costly consequences of having actually lived any One of those lives. Through TV One can skip all the boring, life-wasting parts and experience only the exciting highlights of countless, different lives. With absolute ease One can live many purely rewarding lives throughout Its lifetime. No real, live-It-yourself life can compare to the One, One can live by means of TV. Even more, One can experience things It could never possibly experience in the real, material world, restricted as that world is by laws, both natural and One-made. Through TV One can get to know a lot more about Itself than ever It could by more material means and all absolutely free, or at no apparent cost in life whatsoever.

O: But as One doesn't really do what It watches the Ones on TV doing—or pretending they're doing, as the case more often is—as One doesn't actually live such lives as It sees and hears the Ones on TV living or appearing to live, as One has no part in the world inside the TV set, as It merely watches that world from the world outside, all the experiences One can have through the medium of TV can hardly seem very real to One. In fact, whether One Itself is real or not, whether One exists or not, means nothing to any One or anything in the world of television, except perhaps in Its capacity as just One in a great undifferentiated mass of captivated onlookers—or as a consumer that televised advertising might persuade. As One Itself can hardly be real at all where the world of TV is concerned, how can the world of TV seem very real to One? How can One gain any real understanding of what it is to live any One of those lives It perceives being lived or appearing to be lived on TV? Any experience It can have through TV is bound to lack depth, to seem flat and superficial to One, as though something is missing—some One is missing. Why else would advertisers advertise on television? If the pictures and sounds of the things on TV commercials were enough to satisfy One, there would be no point in advertising on TV, beyond to give every viewer something for nothing. But the purpose of TV commercials is to whet One's appetite for the things on them, not to satisfy It. They're there to make One's life appear flat or deficient by comparison to the life It could be living if It really had such things in Its life.

T: Or if It was right in there with those things, virtually participating in the life or event being acted or played out with them.

O: If One were in virtual reality with such things, you mean?

T: You know of it then? Virtual reality?

O: Only remotely.

T: From television, you mean?

O: Sort of. I haven't experienced it myself. I've seen and heard it described on TV and in books and magazines, and I've seen computer games that take place in virtual realities of a sort. From what I've seen and heard, though, it still has some way to go before it'll be really convincing, and before very many will have access to it.

T: Well, the sooner that happens the better. Then One will really be able to appear to Itself to have all manner of experiences, regardless of the real possibilities, simply by connecting Its senses to a set of information feeds. It'll be able to go anywhere and do anything, and in no time at all, apparently, because everything apparently around One will be able to be and do whatever it must to empower One to appear to Itself to go wherever and do whatever just like that, in nothing flat. One will be able to assume all sorts of roles in all sorts of worlds. And the virtual beings and other things in whatever world It virtually enters will respond or react to It as though It was, in fact, the One It was pretending to be in that world. Virtual reality will be like watching TV from the inside—as an actor in the show, as an insider instead of an outsider. *The* insider, even—the star of the show, the One in the lead role, the One around which the virtual world revolves. And because neither natural nor artificial One-made laws need apply in virtual reality, One will not have to really suffer for any of Its virtual actions, whatever they might be. Not in any deeply inescapable sense.

O: But it won't be real life. One's life will be nothing more than a dream.

T: An extremely real-seeming dream, though. And a whole lot easier and more interesting than any real life One could possibly live.

That's what Nothing can do for One—everything. Everything One could possibly dream of doing with Its life. That's the beauty of the medium of indirect exchange. It doesn't have to be the medium of exchange. It can be the medium of no exchange. No exchange with the real, material world, or even with One's own self. One's own lesser self of course, the part of One that hasn't within Itself to actually do all the things One can possibly dream of doing. Which seems to be all but "the dreamer" part of One. The rest of One seems to exist to make Its life anything but easy—especially realizing a most meaningful life for Itself. The great variety of things One can imagine doing for personal profit might give It an idea of the capacity It has hidden within Itself to find value in being, but thanks to One's other powers for being, even One's power to dream does more to show One what It can't do to make more of Its life than what It can. Most of Its other powers for being One cannot even actually have till It has spent enough of Its precious power to be—Its life, in other words—developing them. As well, One must continue to spend life throughout life to maintain any such power or to develop that power to the greatest possible extent—which is no great extent, as far as extents go. There is a very confining limit to how powerful

One can grow at doing any particular thing. *And* just to top It all off, One is a short-lived being. Not only are the physical capacities of One's body very limited, One exists for what amounts to almost no time at all. As well, One must continue to expend life throughout Its meagre life just to maintain Its capacity to be at all. One must continually see to Its most basic needs.

Then there's everything else besides One's own self to come between One and the realization of Its every dream and the most meaningful being It could possibly know. The world without and about One is not the sort of world to just naturally provide One with all the material things One needs to realize Its dreams. One may well find Itself unable to realize some dream for no other reason than It lacks some worldly something It must have use of to do as It dreams. It may have the physical capacity to do as It dreams, just not all the material somethings It needs to employ that capacity. The thing It is missing may be a thing the world cannot provide of its own entirely natural accord, or it may be something the world, in all its natural fickleness, has not provided where, when and in the amount One requires. Even those relatively few somethings the world just naturally produces One will likely find hard to come by. After all, One does not live in the world alone. One shares the world with other living things, most notably other Ones, each One of whom has the exact same and yet completely different reason for being One has. Because many a One is able to find value in doing the same things One is able to find value in doing, many a One needs many of the same things One needs. The world, alas, contains only so much of anything. Thus One must expend life competing with others for any useful, natural somethings It needs, as well as for the makings of any unnatural somethings It requires—if It has not the free power to obtain either or both at no personal cost to Itself. Beyond that there is the natural tendency of worldly things to wear out or wear away to plague One. Nothing lasts forever, least of all those things of the most use and value to One. The more One uses anything, the faster its matters scatter and the more of what there is in the world to make use and value of must be used up to restore it. And just to make worldly matters worse yet, many of the matters Ones are forced to spread about their worldly place are not the sorts to add to One's health, rather the sorts to take away from It. *And*, as if the world right roundabout One did not offer It little enough, there are all those other worlds, so far away in space that anything they have to offer is more than out of reach so far as One is concerned.

What One has to do, then, to make the most It possibly can of life is find some means to get through everything in Its way, and straightaway, as One hasn't a moment of life to waste. Alas, but everything is so interminably real and all and One's life still so deeply rooted in it all that the best One can do is seem to Itself to go through it all as though there's really nothing at all in Its way. That's where the medium of indirect exchange comes in. It can come between One and everything in Its life that interferes with It in any way and create for It a world where everything, including Itself, is entirely different. Much as it can for One in Its dreams, only more so—much more so even. After all, it's because dreams just aren't real enough that so many Ones find dreams alone insufficient to satisfy them and feel so compelled to do whatever is necessary to realize them. The Nothing stuff of One's dreams seems to serve more to whet One's appetite for life than to satisfy It.

O: Dreams are sort of like TV commercials then.

T: A lot like TV commercials, actually. Like TV commercials, One's dreams send One after the things It needs to really do as It dreams. And, as with the things in TV commercials, those things are usually costly to come by, even if not impossible, owing to everything about One's life. However, with Nothing of a most seemingly real sort working for It, One can seem to really go straight through everything about Itself and realize dream after dream after dream in a steady stream. With the help of tools with the power to make things out of nothing more than the information that renders them most seemingly real to One, without giving them full-bodied being, One can realize for Itself the complete power and freedom to do everything It can possibly dream of doing with Its life.

O: But not really. One still won't be able to actually do any of those things. One's powers won't be real powers.

T: So? Real power isn't always desirable, you know. It means nothing in a world where every tool has been completely freed of the need for any help from any One in fully fulfilling its reason for being. All it can do is needlessly cost One to do anything Itself where there's a tool to do whatever One can do and do it a whole lot faster, better and cheaper than One possibly could. Worse: One would only get in the way of things—especially if One is but One of a world of Ones with as much free life to spend. All the freedom in the world is not near enough to supply each and every One with all the freedom in the world to really do just the *possible* things It can dream of doing with Its life. There just isn't space or materials enough in the real world to empower every One to really do everything It can possibly do to realize value in being. Also, what goes around comes around, which is just another way of saying that because everything in the world is connected to everything else, no One can do anything in the world without interfering with the other Ones and things there. Even possible and permissible things become impossible and impermissible when too many Ones acquire too much freedom to do as they dream with their lives—unless mere information is exploited as a means of providing every One with everything It needs to do as It dreams. Just look at how little words, numbers and pictures can really affect the world. Oh, that's not to say that the stuff they're printed on can't cause upset in the world, if there's very much of it about. But then there needn't be much of it about at all, because information can be encoded on stuff so immaterial as to very nearly not be there at all, on the very stuff of light even. Which also means anything that can be rendered convincingly real by no more than the information that superficially describes it can be multiplied in number very nearly as easily as One can multiply one positive number by another to get a larger number.

O: Or change Its name to a bigger number to make more of Itself.

T: Right! And not only can vast numbers of somethings be made up out of very nearly nothing at all, those somethings can be distributed all over the world in almost no time at all too. One has to look no further than Its television set to see proof of that. By means of TV, something that is nothing more than the description of itself, or a piece of information describing it—a picture of something, say—can be multiplied and broadcast far and wide to great masses of Ones in a matter of seconds. By means of TV, a single picture can easily be worth many thousands of pictures on many thousands of TV screens—enough to make millions and billions even.

Better yet, something doesn't even have to be possible, or even permissible, to be distributed to every One everywhere. There is no natural, unbreakable law that dictates that information must agree with reality. The closest it need come to being based on reality is it must be encoded on real stuff to exist there. Beyond that it can describe absolutely anything that can be described, and thereby introduce any such thing into reality, however impossible or impermissible a fully material version of such a thing might be. In other words, information can beguile. Appearances can deceive—a most fortunate feature of One's existence, given the vast differences between One's power to dream and Its powers to realize Its dreams. One needs all the support It can get to profit from life—even if that support is only a seeming support. And by way of returning to my original point by the long way round, only seeming support is best in a world where too many Ones have too much free life on their minds and hands and not enough material means with which to make good of that life. Not only can there be plenty more for every One, more with which to do everything It could possibly dream of doing, and just like that, in nothing flat, also nothing any One would be able to apparently do would be able to cause any upset in the fully, material world. Just as the things or meanings conveyed by words, numbers and pictures can make no difference in the fully real world unless they cause at least One to act on their behalf in that world, the immaterial things every One uses to do as It dreams could have no effect on that world beyond that which the stuff they are encoded on could have. And that stuff need have no more to do with the things encoded on it than those things have to do with any fully real thing. Indeed, the less either has to do with either, the better. For what One in Its right mind is going to act on information with far too little to do with reality to be at all empowering? Surely such a One is bound not to try anything so pointless and costly as that any more than once. And so long as every One leaves the world alone, the world will leave It alone to see, believe and seem to really do whatever It pleases with Its life. Talk about a dream come true—every dream, in fact. So far as One can see, anyway. And that's far enough for any One. After all, One's life is full of nothing but the mere appearances of things in any case.

Everything that is any real thing to One is only what it appears to One to be. When One perceives anything in the world without and about It, One does not take in the actual thing itself in all its full materiality and depth of being, merely information *about* the thing, information transmitted to It by, say, the light and sound waves exchanged between One and that thing. It is not everything without and about One that is everything to One, but the mere appearance of everything—the information that describes it to One. Information is everything to One—information that has nothing to do with things as they really are. One cannot know anything else for what that thing can be to itself in the midst of everything, only for what it can be to One's own self. One can only perceive anything else from without that thing and from within One's own self. Except for Itself, then, One can only appear to really know anything. Still less, One can see only an infinitesimal fraction of all there is to see around It, and thus can know almost nothing at all about the part any particular thing plays in it all, let alone how it all fits together. So far as One can see, then, all there can really be to it all is It. All else can be but mere appearance and no more. Oneself is the Only thing One can possibly know to the very depths of Its being, the Only thing that can be wholly real to One. And One cannot even really know the One thing It can know, as It really wants to know It, without the completely free power to get to know Itself as fully and deeply as It possibly can—the completely free power that can only be realized by the immaterialization of everything in One's life that stubbornly stands between One and the realization of Its every dream. Immaterialization by means of mere information, that is. Only if mere information can be everything to One—everything One could possibly need to appear to Itself to really do everything It could possibly dream of doing with Its life for whatever valuable reason—can One not only grow to know the full extent of Its potential for realizing value in being, but also realize an absolutely profitable life. Only thus can One engage in a strictly One-sided exchange with the world wherein everything goes One's way and nothing the other, nothing that One is not better off without. Only thus can One escape everything about being here in the world that interferes with One in any way without doing away with Itself and all It could have been to It. Only by means of the medium of indirect exchange can One have It both ways and thereby realize for Itself a life of the greatest quantitative range.

O: For your information, the grippits went that route. They were transported into virtual realities after they ran out of worthwhile things to do in the real world—things that couldn't be done far better, faster and cheaper by their machines. Cheaper in terms of what the grippits had to pay of course. Not cheaper with regards to anything else. In fact, it cost everything else very nearly everything before the grippits were done with it all. Not only did the grippits realize powerful tools far easier and faster than any of the other Ones I heard about, they also went through everything there was in their lives to make good of far easier and faster than the others. And without making all that much of it that I can see. As it wasn't long before a grippit didn't have to pay in any way for any something It desired, it wasn't long before a grippit was not at all driven to appreciate any such thing It acquired for more than the very minimum amount of time. In fact, every grippit soon began needing more and more faster and faster all the time just to remain as pleased as It had been longer before on less.

T: Well, One doesn't desire what It knows nothing about, and it does take One time to discover the valuable possibilities inherent in being Itself in the midst of everything. So even if their machines took no time at all to evolve to the point where they could empower every grippit to do absolutely anything with absolute ease, every grippit's expectations would have had some growing to do, before they would be as great as they could possibly be. As well, the faster a grippit could get everything It could out of anything It could dream of doing to realize value in being, the more dreams It could realize and the fuller and richer Its life could be.

O: But by demanding all the more all the faster all the time, the grippits all but entirely laid waste to the world in the shortest possible time, and all for nothing in the end—nothing any grippit could at all appreciate. Not that any grippit ever found time to care, because every One of them was gassed to death when the two ends of their Horn met—the great Horn of Plenty More they lived in.

T: Oh my. How divinely symbolic—a zero the size of a planet. I assume the grippits' Horn encircled the planet to meet end to end then.

O: That's the impression I got.

T: Now, that's what I call a capital zero—or a Naught with a capital "N."

O: That's what I call a disgraceful waste of an entire world.

T: I take it that, in your estimation, the grippits, for ichthyological troglodytes, were not very logical, not even bright—

O: Ickthy-what?

T: —that, as far as you can see to dream, they missed the whole point of being entirely. But how could they have missed It? After all, they went through everything, including themselves, to realize It. The only way they could have missed It is if It wasn't there at all in the first place.

O: It certainly wasn't there at all in the last place.

T: Oh, but It was. Writ large as a planet—the whole reason for every One of their beings. And that of their tools too. The whole of the sole reason tools are is the whole of the sole reason One is: to make Nothing out of everything so One can make Everything out of nothing—out of One's own self, that is. Everything with a capital "E."

O: Utter nonsense.

T: No. Utter sense. It's the only way One's life can make complete and perfect sense. Why have the power to dream of so much more to be for than simply to exist and not have the power to realize One's dreams? Just to show One's self what a nothing It really is? Just to make One's self the object of a meaningless joke? If One's being here is not to amount to a lot nonsense, the power One wields in the real, material world must be the equal of the power One wields in the worlds of Its dreams. And the only means by which One can realize the completely free and utter power of Its dreams in the real world is by means of Nothing—the same means by which One wields so much free power in Its dreams, only more so. More seemingly real, that is. It is the immateriality inherent in One's dreams that makes everything in them so amenable to One's wishes. Immateriality in the physical sense, of course. One's dreams are most material in the significant sense of the word. After all, it is One's dreams that provide One with more to believe It is for than merely to exist. But it is their immateriality in the corporeal sense that makes them a source of so much seeming power to One. It is because everything in them is no more than the mere appearance of itself that One can do anything It can possibly dream of doing with anything It can possibly dream of, however impossible or impermissible any such act might be in the fully material world—and with complete ease. And ease is as essential to One's being as dreaming is, if One is to make the most of Its life. One's time for being here is just too short and Its powers for being just too meagre for it to make sense to One to give any more of Itself than It absolutely must to the realization of any of Its dreams and any value in being It might thus realize. Only One who can, with complete ease, do anything It can possibly dream of doing with Its life for whatever profitable reason can realize not only a purely profitable being, but all It possibly can out of life. Only such a One as that can discover all It has within Itself to be to Itself, all It can possibly mean to Itself.

O: But what about everything else? What about the other Ones in One's life?

T: What about them—if One can do without them? Or at least seem to.

O: I refuse to believe that Ones are meant to live oblivious of each other.

T: Well, they certainly aren't meant to live together as One. Any fool can see that. Especially the One you met up with. Or at least It could, if It was still here to see anything. But It's not, because of other of the Ones without and about It. Only some One or Ones behind the powerful tools every One used could have driven those tools to behave as they did toward the fool.

When there's no longer anything of any value One can actually do for any One else, there is only one thing left One can do for any One else, and that is be or mean less than It. And who wants to do that for any One else? No One in Its right mind, right? It's no wonder, then, that Ones do their best to escape any and all associations with each other as much and as fast as possible. They're only lucky their tools aren't driven to be superior to them. But then they are, aren't they?—by Ones themselves, to save themselves from themselves and everything else about them.

In the beginning, it is even more difficult for One to live without other Ones than it is for One to live with them. One has too little power to mean—to make a difference in things—without them. In concert with others, though, One's is a different story. Amazing, that: how individually Ones can add up to nothing and yet en masse can add up to considerably more. It's the only instance I know of in reality where nothing multiplied however many times can equal anything—at least until the tools have been realized that can render it nothing en masse as well. But then it no longer matters how little it all can amount to, because then there's Nothing to being Everything to One's own self. The only other Ones One need associate with then are those It can have completely free and utter power over—the merely seemingly real Ones Its tools can summon into existence for It to use however It pleases and send completely away the moment One has easily got all It can out of being with them.

That's how the grippits must have both stayed and gone as far as they did, before they left this here plane of being entirely. They must have freed themselves from their obvious dependence on each other's meagre, needful powers so much and so fast there just wasn't time for it to enter their minds to make any of their tools at all demanding to use for any One of them.

O: Or time for them to make much of the fully material world either.

T: So? There wasn't much of anything to it to begin with, was there? If there had been a good deal more than the almost nothing there just naturally was, the grippits wouldn't have needed the help of so many powerful tools to make their lives sufficiently worthwhile. Their own meagre physical powers would have been sufficient to avail them of all the things they needed to do as they dreamed with their lives. But it wasn't like that, was it? For any of the Ones you met or heard about. Every One of them had come to be just to find Itself consumed of a dreamy need to be given so much and living in world with almost no give at all to it. What with all the material proof there was in their lives of the absurdity of their being and being able to dream of so much more to be for than simply to be, it's a wonder they didn't all just go mad right then and be done with it. They didn't, though. Instead they joined their meagre, needful powers for being in one great unified effort to change themselves, as much and as fast as possible, from have-naughts into have-Naughts, or from beings who individually had no real power to make much of their lives into beings who individually apparently had the completely free and utter power to be absolutely meaningful. Unfortunately, though, they didn't all make it all the way to The End of their lives—to their ultimate reason for being, that is. Only the grippits succeeded in apparently immaterializing everything about themselves and making Everything they possibly could of themselves before they left here entirely. The money machine succeeded in immaterializing everything about Itself, but so much so as to leave Itself too little to live on here after leaving. For long, certainly. And though the fool was on the right track, It got bumped off entirely before It reached The End of that track by the insufficient immaterialization of the role of Ones in One another's life.

And now that The Mystery of mysteries has been solved—that of "Why life?"—and just like that, in Nothing flat, the only thing that remains to be discovered is where you yourself will go from here? Will you stay or leave entirely? It would be a shame for you to just altogether stop being here after having come so far so fast from here. You don't want to cease to be entirely, do you? Not yet?

O: Of course not.

T: You still want to be *and* leave here then.

O: Yes. I mean no. I want to leave here. I don't want to be here.

T: But you can't do that. You have to have it both ways—unless all you want is out of here. If all you want is out of here, then all you have to do is disappear entirely. You have only to cease to be here at all. But if you still want to make it to The End of your life here, you've but One final step to take to make Everything of yourself. And from the looks of the landscape, you've taken half of It already. Still, I cannot help but wonder how exactly you're going to manage that last half step, what with what you've got left to go on. It's obvious the tools necessary to empower you to feel entirely out of place here have been put in your place. But you've no virtual realities to completely lose and find yourself in. Not just yet, anyway. That's not to say you can't still make Everything of yourself. Only that you'll have to do so on less than the grippits made Everythings of their selves on. You'll have to do so on dreams you dream up yourself without any outside help. But that should be no problem for One who's gone so far so fast from here as you have. You should be able to believe absolutely in yourself in no more time than it takes to count from Eight to Ten. After that your dreams will be absolutely real to you and you will have gone even farther from being here than the grippits did before they left entirely.

O: All right. That's enough, Two. Open the door.

T: Door? What door?

O: The door you're sticking through.

T: [*Two backs up to disappear from view behind the door.*] I'm not sticking through any door. Or around here any more.

O: Don't you leave me, Two! Not without unlocking this door!

[*Two calls the following lines to One as Its voice gradually fades into the distance beyond the door. Between bouts of listening at the door, One alternates between yanking on the door handle and pounding on the door while yelling at Two to come back and open the door.*]

What with the difference between
One's power to dream of more
And Its means to realize dreams
And be what It is for,
That must be free which has a price,
If One's to leave and stay behind;
Dark must be light and black be white,
If One's to lose and keep Its mind.

Yes, if One's absurdly costly life
Is to make whole and perfect sense,
What's wrong with It must be as right
And all at no expense.

Everything And Nothing

Dreams must be Reality
And the least the most of all,
If the smallest number is to be
The reason for It All.

One must save Its life and live It too.
It must be and not be here
To have Its cake and eat it too
While neither disappears.
One must have It both ways,
Coincidentally in time,
To live a life that only pays
Despite the price in Its design.

Only words, pictures and numbers
And such things as fill One's dreams
Can facilitate such wonders
As cannot be by deeper means.
And a mind that roams among such things
As are and yet are not
Is a mind that, in Its wanderings,
Remains both here and not.

Only that which no more than reflects
The meaning to be found
Amidst things of deep effect
Can turn One's life around.
The mere appearance of reality
Must thoroughly suffice,
If One's to simply start to be
To achieve Its End in life.

For when everything is feigned
Of the Nothing stuff of dreams,
Every thing's the same,
However different it seems,

And thus can easily be changed
Into any other thing,
Much as money is exchanged
For so many other things.

It's as if the stuff of greatness
Were no more than quantity
And the means of knowing greatness
No more than ease and speed.
No wonder Nothing's all It's all about—
The End of everything.
Only One plus Nothing can amount
To All of everything.

And now you finally know The End,
You must most easily see
How One plus Zero equals Ten
Or any other quantity.
Indeed, I wonder as I wander
Through the moments till we part
How great will grow your number
When you play The Whole Part.

Nine will give you time to clear your mind
Of whatever still is here
With any power to undermine
Your power to appear
Absolutely capable
Of believing any dream
To be absolutely possible
For One of your mere means.

And the time, I see, is nearly Nine,
When you must be on your way.
These then are my final lines:
Just so you'll never say

That Two never did Nothing for you,
I do for you this thing:
I give you this clue to see you through
And leave you with Nothing . . .

O: [*Yells after Two.*] Well? What clue? [*Puts ear tight to door.*]

T: [*Whispers in One's ear from just beyond the door.*] Have you tried the wall?

O: The wall? [*Steps to one side to stand before the wall. Reaches out to touch the wall only to find that the further It reaches the more of Its hand disappears into its blackness. Before One has time to fully react to Its discovery, the door flies open and slams into the back of One, sending It into the wall entirely.*]

Nine

[*One thrashes about looking for a handhold, a foothold—something to orient Itself with . . .*

. . . nothing. Not even hands and feet that One can see: only feel—and feel nothing but nothing with. Realizing that It is only struggling with Itself, One stops—and thinks.]

Odd that: that I'm not more upset than I am. I've just lost everything—everything but life Itself—and I'm not paralyzed with fear and loss. Indeed, not since the beginning of this madness have I been especially upset. Taken aback, yes, quite taken aback. But not overly upset. And that doesn't make sense.

Not unless what Two said makes sense. And I can't see that. I can't believe that my whole reason for being has been to discover that the world, in fact, is utterly flat—and ultimately, that it doesn't exist at all. Except in my own mind. I'd rather see myself as having been in such a hurry to go through it all that I didn't see the end up ahead and sailed right off the edge into nothing at all. At least then I'd have

. . . nothing. Not even hands and feet that One can see: only feel—and feel nothing but nothing with.

something to look back on. The other way, I not only have nothing to look forward to but back on as well. Nothing but a lot of meaningless dreams.

Actually, when I think about it, it's only because of the things One can look back on that It can look forward to anything. Or in other words, One cannot dream up something—anything even—out of nothing. When One dreams It dreams of the perceptible differences other things have made in Its life, the effects they have had on It—the colors, shapes, sounds, smells and so forth they have caused One to perceive of. One weaves Its dreams out of memories of sensations It has realized through being with other things. It never dreams up anything out of nothing, let alone something. Certainly not in the significant sense of the word "something"—a thing, that is, with the power to empower One to make more of Its life than mere existence. Before One can even so much as dream of more to be for than simply to exist, It must have discovered something of the deep value that might be realized from being with certain other things, from interacting with them. It must have at least an inkling of the invigorating fullness of being It might come to know with help from without Itself.

By means of the mere stuff of dreams—by means of information, that is—we Ones have realized for ourselves the closest means we've known yet of realizing something out of nothing in the physical sense. We've come the closest we've ever come to materializing something—anything—out of utterly empty space. And by such means we have also come the closest we've come to realizing the power of One's dreams in the deeply real world. It is because the things in the worlds of One's dreams are made of nothing more than the information that renders them merely apparent to One that One can make the most unlikely things, even impossible things, come to be more freely and easily in those worlds than the most likely things can happen in the deeply real world outside One's head. Not being so deeply committed to being themselves as deeply real things are, such things are free to be made to behave in whatever way One might have a mind to make them behave. The same goes for the things contained in novels, movies, video games and such. Because the things embodied in such informational entertainments are only superficially real, they can be manipulated with the same free and utter power One wields in Its dreams. Potentially, they can be made to do anything any One can imagine doing with them—to realize any sort of world. Even—or rather, ever—better, the power to enter other worlds far removed from the context of One's existence in the deeply real world is becoming more and more seemingly real all the time, as not only our information tools but also our more physical tools grow ever more capable of intervening for One on behalf of Its dreams. The time is faster and faster approaching when One will be able to realize no end of deep value in being out of very little more than information alone; a power much on the order of that of being able to live a full life on money alone, or pure numbers; the former, though, able to empower One to easily avail Itself of the greatest variety as well as the greatest quantity in life. One will be able to obtain and use the greatest variety of things to do the greatest variety of things in life and all with the greatest ease and speed—even to realize Its dreams even as It dreams them. Or at least seem to really do so.

Or will it? Will the promise of all that power really turn out to be as empowering as it promises to be? For that matter, is all the power we are realizing even now by informational means really as empowering as it appears to be? The growing power to transmit and receive information to and from everywhere in almost no time at all does empower One to encounter more and more worldly things during the course of Its limited life than It is capable of encountering firsthand. Even so, One can still take in only so much at a time. The only way It can take in more and more is by skimming faster and faster over everything. Alas, but a glimpse of any particular thing does not make for an understanding of it. In fact, it does not make much, if anything at all, of that thing. Like the split-second flash of a camera, it captures a mere instant in the existence of the thing and frames walls around that instant that isolate it from everything that led to it and all that followed or will follow from it. And that applies to other Ones every bit as much as it does to any of the other things in One's life.

One may be able to exchange being with more and more Ones in more and more places by means of ever-newer-and-better information tools, but only if those Ones are not too busy paying heed to other things and will pay heed to One—or One Itself is not too busy meeting more immediate and pressing demands on Its own attention. Inevitably, One ends up talking and listening to a growing number of tools as more and more Ones attempt to spread themselves around more and more by such means. As is always the case, though, with any fixed quantity, the more it is spread around, the less of it there is anywhere. The more things—that includes other Ones—One is bent on involving in Its life, the less involved One can be with each thing, or the more remote and fleeting—the more superficial—must One's involvement with each thing be, if One is to fit every one into the constraints of Its life. Even the Ones One is physically closest to cannot but lose their depth of meaning for One, just as One can only do for them. Others are bound to see little, if any, point in regarding One, who only remotely and minimally involves Itself with them, as any more than a small and insignificant part of their lives.

Indeed, the most immediate and familiar of things—those things with the power to most profoundly affect One's life the quickest—are unlikely to be able hold a candle to the strange and amazing things to be seen in distant places, when One can look in on the latter as quickly and easily as It can the former. Nor is One bound to restrict Its attention to the deeply real, when It can achieve perceptual satisfaction through the less material means of Its information tools. Because information can have only the merest connection to the deeply real world, it can convey to One things and events well beyond the capacity of One's deep reality to accommodate in fully embodied form—at least without causing great disruption. Anything goes, when it comes to information. Anything is possible and nothing impossible with the power of information. Even previously forbidden pastimes—forbidden by natural or One-made law. In fact, such pastimes are bound to develop an almost mesmerizing power to attract One's attention. As One is rendered more and more able to seem to really indulge Its every possible whim at no personal cost by the increasing power to manufacture anything out of nothing more than information for One's seemingly real use in whatever It can dream of doing, there is less and less to prohibit or even discourage One from indulging Itself in every possible respect and more and more to compel It to do so. After all, it is nothing less than the chance to see One's self in a whole new and utterly powerful light—even if that light is bound not to remain all that strong. Not for long anyway. Acts deemed impermissible or impossible by the more material standards of One's existence tend to become almost too easy for One when drained of their fearful power to inflict profound costs on One by their conversion to purely informational form. Such acts do not only acquire an increasing attractiveness then, they also lose their capacity to amaze or shock much faster, forcing One to continually go to ever-greater extremes in such acts to achieve the same level of excitement It achieved before at lower levels of lawlessness.

To be sure, we Ones have always dabbled in forbidden pastimes, but mostly in the privacy of our own minds, where the rest of the deeply real world, including other Ones, could not interfere with us—cost us, that is. Many a One's fear of losing the powerful assistance of others or of inciting them to use their combined powers against It has discouraged It from treating others with utter disrespect. The fear of similar retaliation by the rest of the deeply real world has also given many a One good reason not to flaunt Its power to imagine exhibiting a complete disregard for it. Our powerful information tools have changed all that, however—the capacity, that is, of the deeply real to keep our imaginations at bay. Or at least it would appear they have, judging from so much of what we are showing and telling ourselves through our tools of mass communication. With the help of those tools we are more and more replacing the old awareness of One's deep dependency on other worldly Ones and things for increased certainty of survival and quality of life with a new, free and fearless awareness—the awareness that nothing stands in any One's way anymore, that anything is possible where One is concerned.

Though it is true that things made of no more than the information that superficially describes them need be no more subject to the restrictions of the real, material world than the things of One's dreams, such things can greatly affect the deeply real world—indeed, must—if enough of that world is enlisted on their behalf, even if only to give them something to be painted, printed or encoded on. Alas, but there are other more effective ways to litter the world with noxious matters than spreading papers, inks, plastics and so forth about the place. The natural entropic tendency of our more physical tools to spread the remains of spent fuels and materials throughout the things we and other worldly things physically live on is not the only way by which hazardous substances might be leaked increasingly into the worldly living space. The mesmerizing ease with which we can perform all manner of deeds in our dreams and by other insubstantial means may also pose a substantial threat to the capacity of the world to support life and quality of life. We Ones, being the fully embodied things we are, cannot help but affect each other and the rest of the world with our actions—especially if our actions are facilitated by powerful tools. And we act based on what we know and believe about the world around us, and what we know and believe is based on the information we take in, however accurate or inaccurate that information might be with regard to the deeply real world. Of course, the less that information has to do with things as they really deeply are, the less likely we are to have the effect on the world we expect to have. We could even end up threatening our very existence with our behaviour, as well as our potential for making more of our lives besides.

At present we are using the growing power of our information tools to give ourselves no end of reason to keep working to buy as much as possible of an ever-faster growing assortment of increasingly powerful goods that cost less and less to realize—or so it seems. But then the greater grows our tools' portion of the work of rearranging the natural things of the world into the things of our shared Dream and the smaller grows our own portion, the more it seems to us that somethings materialize in the world out of nothing and nowhere at all. Nor does the indirect means we must increasingly rely on for a view of the ever-faster changing world around and increasingly beyond us all do much to undermine that impression. Between our increasingly small and remote involvement in the worldly goings-on behind it all and information that focuses our attention on the ever-increasing varieties and quantities of increasingly inexpensive somethings being realized in the world to the exclusion of most everything else, it is no wonder worldly things of a deeper order fade further and further from every One's mind. Soon they will seem very little more than the ghostly remains of forgotten dreams. Nor are the somethings realized from them long for the world of our minds either. They too are fading faster and faster from our minds and our lives to make room for yet more and more such things. Increasingly, they seem little more substantial than the flashy, fleeting images that first introduce them to us.

All that insubstantiality, that immateriality, is only skin deep, though. It is only merely apparent—as are the falling prices on everything. Indeed, in light of all that actually goes into realizing all those somethings, their falling prices are not so much falling prices as demeaning and degrading prices. Considering the amount of precious worldly materials that go into realizing such things relative to how much they are appreciated—before they are tossed aside to add further and faster to the ever-growing problem of waste disposal, as well as to make room for still more—those things are becoming increasingly expensive, not decreasingly expensive.

Then there's all the life involved in realizing all those somethings—or in not realizing the potential value in them. Our increasingly powerful tools may be empowering us to realize more and more somethings, which cost us less and less life to supply and buy. Still, the more somethings One must acquire, however low their prices, the more life It must spend working to earn enough to buy them all, even to the point where It has no life to spare for actually putting any of the goods It buys to good and gainful use. Then what good is any of Its goods to It? Of what value is Its own life to It? None, if not even the work It spends so much of Its life doing is any more than a means of getting the money It needs to buy goods It has neither the time nor the energy to really use in making more of Its life. One, then, is little more than a mere tool to Itself—a thing whose reason for being is to realize a lot of potentially valuable things it does not itself have the capacity to appreciate. Still less, as One must perceive Itself to be not as well off as It could be to see Itself as able to be better off than It is—because It must perceive Its life to be deficient in some respect to see any point in trying to realize the means to fill that deficiency—and because One can hold only so much in mind at any one time, One who can see no end of ways and means by which Its life might be made sufficient is also One who cannot see what It has realized in life for what It has not realized. It is One who can never see what It has gained or achieved for what It has not yet gained or achieved. It is One who cannot but spend Its life running in vicious, empty circles round and round Itself like a power tool possessed of no more reason for being than to go through its motions.

Evidently, the growing power to realize more and more things of potential use and value out of the stuffs of the world does not necessarily imply the growing power to make more and more of life. Nor does the growing power to realize more and more out of less and less in the physical sense necessarily imply the growing power to make more and more out of life in the significant or meaningful sense of the word "more." How is that so? Easy, that's how. After all, ease is all it's all about, or at least the means to all it's all about: more, and ultimately, the most—the greatest of ease in acquiring and using every kind of something any One could possibly dream of in making more of One's life. Or so we would have ourselves believe, judging from so much of the information we share amongst ourselves by means of the tools of mass communication. The reality behind it all, though, suggests that making the most of One's life is not as simple as that. Really, there is more to making the most of One's life than getting everything free and doing everything with the absolute of ease.

Indeed, for a being such as One to realize everything It could possibly desire out of life at no apparent cost to Itself whatsoever, It would have to realize a power very like the One It wields in the worlds of Its dreams. The worlds of One's dreams are strictly One-way worlds, or worlds where One is the only thing with a being of Its own and One's will the only law. They are worlds where One is only apparently involved in being with anything but Itself. A power in the real world like the completely free and utter power One enjoys in Its dreams would have to equally un-involve One in being with everything around It to demand so very little of One in return for so very much. And how could a power in which One played only the most superficial part—no deeper role than that of dictatorial spectator—empower One to realize any deep significance in being? What justification would One have for considering Itself an integral part of that power? After all, it would not be as though One would even have to be mindful of Its exercise of that power. One who had nothing at all to lose from anything It did would need be no more conscious of Its actions than It was in Its sleep. It would not need to give any careful thought to anything It did with anything. Nor would It have any reason to see any of the things It employed in doing as It dreamed as anything special. From Its unassailable position of absolute power over and above everything—where nothing could touch It in any profoundly meaningful way that could not be soon taken utterly for granted by One—One would be only too free to regard the vast variety of the seemingly embodied without and about It as just so many "things." Everything about One's life would all too soon become blunted and blurred into a flat and meaningless background against which not even One Itself could stand out for any appreciable time as anything special. For how important can anything be that means nothing to anything else of any importance whatsoever? Amidst a vast variety of things powerless to make any more than the merest of differences in One's life, there can be nothing by which to gage the greatness of One's life but the sheer number of experiences One is able to pack into a lifetime. And if quantity, pure and simple, is all One's life is really about, One might as well just spend It counting sheep in Its sleep and leave out the sheep. Either that or do like the money machine and pursue endless quantities of free money whose value has nothing whatsoever to do with anything worldly.

One's dreams do give One Its direction in life, Its reason for being—something more to believe It is for than simply to strive to survive in a world that does not essentially care whether One is even there or not. For One, the power to dream is the seemingly preternatural power to see Its life in a different context, to see the circumstances of Its existence as other than they actually are, and even how they might be if One can find the way to render them thus. One's power to dream, then, *is* integral to the potential It has for realizing a deep sense of value in being. It is just not *all* there is to One's power to realize a deeply meaningful life. Far from it—as far as everything is from nothing.

Only One who has acquired a knowledge of being in the world deep in the midst of everything has things worth pondering and playing with in those otherworldly worlds within Itself where anything can happen, anything One can possibly imagine. One's dreams are full of things One has encountered either directly or indirectly in the deeply real world where things are through and through themselves—except, of course, for those things whose realities go no deeper than the information that superficially describes them. Even the latter owe their existences as much to the worldly stuff their descriptions are painted, printed or encoded on as to any imaginative effort on any One's part to dream them up and give them material being outside Its brain. And like anything else any One has imagined, they exist at all only by virtue of the fully embodied—the deeply real. However truly new and strange might seem the things of One's dreams, they are but concoctions of things and parts of things One has come to know through Its existence deep in the midst of everything.

Any meaning any such thing has for One it has only by virtue of what its full-bodied counter-part or -parts can mean to One. Even the dreamy freedom and ease with which One can make all manner of mundane things behave in strange, improbable ways is significant to One only by virtue of the fact that One is far from free to do such things so easily in the real, material world.

Unlike the inner "otherworlds" of One's dreams where One is the only thing with a being of Its own and One's will the only law, the deeply real world of One's being is chock-full of all manner of things with beings of their own, every one of which has a say in the running of things simply by virtue of being wholly part of it all. One is just one of an unimaginably vast and complex assemblage of fully embodied things, with all the rights to make a difference in that assemblage accorded any fully embodied thing possessed of the same physical size and powers One has. No wonder the difficulty One has in making Its dreams come fully true. In the deeply real world, One can do rather like It can in Its dreams and take things and make different things out of them. It can even put things together in unnatural combinations—that's to say, combinations they are unlikely to assume on their own. However, It cannot force things to become what they do not have within themselves to realize together. And the less likely things are to just naturally become something—the less prone they are to become such a thing on their own—the harder and more costly it is bound to be for One to make them become such a thing—and to stay that thing. Nor are the results of realizing such a thing bound to be as simple and straightforward as they are in One's dreams. What with how everything is directly or indirectly connected to everything else in the deeply real world, any difference One makes there is bound to have deeper, more penetrating results than it had in any imaginary world within One. Nothing One does in Its head goes beyond Its head unless One sees that it does. Everything One does in the deeply real world touches many more things than just those One uses to accomplish the act. Nothing any One could ever dreamily wish for, then, could ever be as simple in the deeply real world as it is in the superficial world of Its dreams. Which is why no One should ever trust too much in Its dreams. That and the fact that One depends on the deeply real world for Its very power to be, as well as Its powers to know and dream and realize dreams.

The world without and about One may be able to amount to more than just everything in it because such as One inhabits it—a being with the power to know and dream of more to be for than simply to exist in the world. All the same, it is only by virtue of those things in the world around One with the power to help One realize a profound sense of worth that One can even begin to know of greater reasons for being than simply to survive. It is only because value of a more deeply meaningful sort than the purely quantitative kind is already one of the things One can realize out of being in the world with other worldly things that One can make Its life amount to more than just the sum of the things participating in It. However much One might rearrange the things of the world into things of greater use to It in realizing life and more besides, It does not create somethings out of nothings. What It does is realize somethings out of somethings that *can* be.

Meaning derives from the participation of things in one another's being—from the exchange between them of the power to make differences in each other's existence. And because meaning derives from the power of things to be for each other—to mean to each other—nothing meaningful can exist in isolation. And that applies as much to One as to anything else. More so than to a lot of other things, in fact, because One cannot even so much as remain alive without a lot of help from outside Itself. One deeply depends on things in the world without and about It for Its very life, as well as everything about Itself—on things with beings of their own. Not the least of which are other Ones, without whose help One could make very little difference to Itself or anything else. Indeed, the considerable added power One now has to survive and make more out of life is the result of the expenditure of a good deal of life by a good many Ones both past and present in wrestling with the problem of more than merely being in a world little given to revealing its hidden helpful nature.

Still, for all the differences we Ones have made in the world and in our own lives, we have not changed the essential nature of the world, or of ourselves. In a sense, the differences we have made in the world and in ourselves are superficial, or more apparent than real. And nothing has done more to make those differences appear real than the growing power of our tools to empower us to realize somethings out of mere information. While the ever more for ever less we are thus able to realize does wonders to strengthen our belief in the growing reality of our power to materialize things of use and value out of utterly empty space, it does not render our belief any truer for all the stronger it makes it. For despite all the added power we have realized, every single One of us is still as deeply dependent as ever on the deeply real world for Its very life, as well as everything in It—including the information with which It knows and dreams. Knowledge, that most fundamental of tools, might appear to be quite immaterial if One considers knowledge in isolation: that seemingly immaterial something that makes up the difference between an unknowing mind and the same mind made knowledgeable. Even so, One's knowledge exists as much by virtue of the things about One that One can grow to know about as by virtue of One being there at all to grow to know about anything. One's is a knowledge of bodies, as well as a body of knowledge—an embodied knowledge of embodied things—whether it is firsthand knowledge or knowledge others have passed onto One of their own firsthand encounters with other wholly real things. It is a knowledge of the differences fully embodied things can make in one another's existence—the things they can be together, the things they can mean together. And it is of such knowledge—such things—that One's dreams are made. Indeed, One cannot even imagine the power and freedom to realize any sort of value in being without envisioning deeply real things—or at least things dreamt up out of deeply real things—with which It could free and empower Itself to realize that value. And of course, if It cannot avail Itself of the things It needs to do as It dreams, either because such things have been lost for some reason or cannot be fully realized in the world, then the most One can do is talk or dream of what It might have done with Its life had It only had the necessary material means to do so. And if It cannot even obtain those fully embodied things It needs to survive, then One cannot even so much as dream of what It would do with Its life. Not for long certainly.

For all that mere information might empower One to know and dream of, it cannot, in deeply real fact, empower One on its own, under its own power alone. Indeed, it is only by virtue of what One and other of the things in the fully real world can be and mean together that it can empower One to know and dream of anything. Any power information has to be deeply meaningful to One it has only by virtue of the deeply real things with the power to touch One in profoundly penetrating ways. Therefore information that serves to render One unaware or unconscious of Its deep dependencies and vulnerabilities in regards to other fully real things actually serves more to undermine One's power to know deep meaning in being than to add to It in any way.

Even if we Ones were able to contain within acceptable limits any deeply real costs that devolved from the widespread disregard for the deeply real world that would all too likely attend a strong and pervasive belief in One's power to realize Its every dream with help from next to nothing at all, we would then find ourselves only too free to take that world utterly for granted. It would then be within our seeming power to look down on everything worldly and to view any value imparted to our lives by any such things as simply our due—or even to demean and devalue that worth by regarding it as too lowly or base to be worthy of our deep appreciation. As such small-minded Ones, we would not contribute much, if at all, to the more made of the world, for all we might use up of the potential we shared with it. Nor would we be likely to make much of our own lives, for all our sense of self-empowerment and -importance, for there would be nothing about to make anything of our lives with, so far as we were concerned.

A picture may be worth a thousand words, but is it worth One's life? Visions of a safe, clean and caring world only available in One's mind or in pictures can do little, if anything, for One. The most they can supply One with is the mere, shallow pretence of a meaningful life, and only if One can at least be guaranteed of receiving from the world those deeply real things It must have to remain alive. One can no more live on words or pictures alone than It can on pure numbers alone. It can no more live on the mere appearances of things, however seemingly real, than It can on dreams alone. Not even just mindfully. Not a deeply meaningful life. Therefore the only information One is really justified in entrusting with Its life is information that will invest One with a material knowledge, material in both the physical and the significant sense of the word "material."

It is not enough that One simply know of the valuable differences certain worldly things can possibly make in Its life. One must also know what things those things come from and what costs are likely to result from their realization. Indeed, it is the cost of something that determines whether it is really something or not—too little as well as too much cost. One is still a being of limited powers with a limited time for being—despite any appearances to the contrary. Where One is concerned, then, there is such a thing as too much of a good thing, or too many good things, just as there is too little or not enough. There is an end to the added value One can realize in the space of a lifetime, an end beyond which One cannot get more out of life, but less. Therefore the trick to making the most of One's life not only involves figuring out how to get the most for any life One spends, but also involves knowing when One is asking too much for too little.

At the very least, everything in One's life costs It life to realize. And though we Ones have found ways to lengthen the average life span, we have not lengthened It by all that much. Certainly not by so much that One can afford to waste much of It on meaningless pursuits. Not even the pursuit of the means to save life can have any meaning, if it leaves no time to live a life worth living. The same is equally true of the pursuit of the means to make more of life. Though we Ones cannot make more of our lives without the things we need to do as we dream with our lives, it takes more than just filling the world with things with the potential to be useful to us in realizing value in being to make more of the world and our lives. There is more to value, where One is concerned, than can be accounted for by simply totalling the number of useful things One went through during Its lifetime. Indeed, it is questionable whether such an adjective as "useful" can even be used to describe things that only empower One to realize the mere numerical pretence of a meaningful life. To actually realize the potential something has to be useful to One in realizing value out of life, One must not only use that thing, but actually appreciate the usefulness of it as well. Potential value that goes unrealized is not real value. It is only value that could have been, had One only been able to realize it. To realize the value of our somethings, we have to actually value them and the things we are able to do with them. And we cannot deeply appreciate anything without maintaining a deep respect for the world on which we depend for it: a respect we shouldn't find hard to maintain, given that the world every One of us so deeply depends on for everything is a world not only possessed of a limited supply of deeply real things, but also one in which every one of those things is directly or indirectly connected to every other in one great seething mass of change. It should be easy for One to have a care with regard to worldly affairs in a world like that. All too easy—if not enough Ones do their respective parts to help make the most, or even just more, of the potential for deep greatness we share so deeply with One another and the rest of the world. Caring may not be easy. Indeed, it can be quite a costly capacity, inflicting such things as fear, pain and loss on One. All the same, it is One's power to care that invests One's other powers for being—Its powers to know and dream and realize dreams—with whatever power they have to be profoundly meaningful to One. No One can make more of the world and Its life without mindfully involving Itself enough in that world—without giving more than just Its life, Its existence, in return.

The potential for more is there—or here rather—within us and everything roundabout us. Even the potential for us to make the most of everything. So, too, is the potential for us to make nothing out of what more there could have been. That more can be is no guarantee that it will be. It is not inevitable. It will not simply happen for us. Not even by means of powerful tools, if those tools render insignificant, even if only in our own minds, those things without, about and throughout us all to which we are so deeply indebted for our very lives and everything in them. For there to be more than the merest more to being, then, there must be more to seeing than simply seeing. One must see deep into Its being—to the other things that be, the things It so deeply depends on for Its very power to be, as well as Its powers for knowing, dreaming and realizing dreams. One must give as well as take part in the great exchange of meaning, the great interplay of being. One must care enough to think and think enough to care.

[A BLINDING FLASH!]

Ten

Whatever are you doing?!

One: TWO! [*Squinting from beneath the shelter of Its raised hand at the glaring, three-headed apparition hovering over It.*] And Three and Four, it looks like. What are you doing here?

Two: What are *we* doing here?! What are *you* doing here?! You're supposed to be dreaming and you were *thinking,* of all things. You're absolutely free to dive right in and do absolutely anything you can dream of doing, and you're still acting as though you have to stop and consider a thing before you do it. Do you know how ridiculous that is? Worse—what a waste of life that is?

O: Nothing like the ridiculous waste of life this is—being mired in all this Nothing.

T: Mired? You're absolutely free of everything. There's no ground to push you up, no gravity to pull you down, nothing you have to make your way around, or over or under—nothing to interfere with you in any way. You're afloat on pure freedom.

Whatever are you doing?!

O: I am not. This isn't floating, and it certainly isn't freedom. It's not anything at all.

T: My, but you're an especially poor excuse for a dreamer, aren't you?

O: No. Not especially. I love to dream and fantasize as much as the next One. Or at least I did until I ended up here—and not here. Now I can't see any point in dreaming. There's nothing about me to point the way.

T: Of course not. That's entirely up to you now.

O: No, it's not. It can't be—because my power to dream is not mine alone. I'm not all there is to It. There's a whole lot more involved in my being able to dream than just me. There are all those things that can touch me in ways I can't simply forget—other things with beings of their own. I can't dream or mean without them.

T: You only think you can't is all, and all because you stopped and thought instead of just losing yourself in your dreams like you were supposed to.

O: But that's just It. I'm not supposed to lose myself; I'm supposed to find myself. I'm supposed to find out what more I can be to myself than simply alive, and I can't do that without being with more than just me.

T: Oh my. That sounded serious.

O: I *am* serious.

T: How did the likes of you ever get as far from here as this then? You're obviously not "The **1**ndividual" we took you for. (That's spelt with a capital **ONE**, in case you didn't get that. Which, no doubt, you didn't, actually being anything but the consummate **1**ndividual we believed you to be.) **O**ne plus **N**othing can equal **E**verything, given the right **ONE**. But you couldn't even make One plus Zero equal Ten. Obviously, you're not the right sort at all. You've no right at all to not be here like this.

O: I couldn't agree with you more. And here I thought I'd never see the day—or night—when you and I were of the same mind.

T: To think we mistook your disagreeable nature for just your **1**ndividuality. To think we believed it was just your determination to be a self-made **ONE** speaking, when, in fact, it was the voice of just another commonplace one we were hearing—that's a one with the befitting lower case "o" we'll have you know. You're no **1**ndividual. You're not destined for greatness, least of all the greatest of greatness. You have none of what it takes to be that great.

O: Not now, certainly. Now that you've taken me for everything I had to make anything of myself with. As for "The **1**ndividual" or "Self-made **ONE**" you speak so highly of, It's just a myth. No such thing can exist. No One is or can be a world unto Itself.

T: Trust a commoner to say such a thing, especially one possessed of so lowly and common a sense as the one you sport.

O: As opposed to the highly specialized sense of self you would have me swear by. For that is all you're peddling—specialization. Only you're not suggesting specialization for the sake of sharing the burden of realizing meaningful lives in a vast and highly complex world. Quite the contrary. You're suggesting specialization solely and wholly for the sake of One's own self. And not even that, if One really thinks about It. **1**ndividualism taken to the extreme you suggest would have the same effect on One extreme specialization would have. By specializing utterly on getting to know Itself, One would end up knowing about a part of reality so small as to be the equivalent of nothing at all in relation to all there is to know about, just as One would who devoted Its entire life to studying just one of the innumerable, infinitesimal parts of reality and utterly ignored all the rest. Extreme specialization can only narrow One's knowledge of existence to a tiny point of light amidst an intricate vastness One can know nothing about, nor even see for the single, solitary star by which It steers Its way through Its narrow, little, light-tight life.

T: That sounds more like an argument for **1**ndividualism than one against It. After all, it's not as though One can really know much in any case, is it? Nor is Its power of imagination anything to boast to the great overwhelming "all" about. Indeed, that One can even imagine such a thing as "The **1**ndividual" or "The self-made **ONE**" just goes to show how very small and short-sighted the power in One's dreams really is, for all the apparent utter-ness of it. It is only too natural for One to imagine Itself as somehow separate from everything else, when, in fact, It is profoundly part of something vastly greater than anything It or any One else could possibly imagine. So why bother even trying? Why not just let the only seemingly endless power in One's dreams go completely to One's head? Why not be Everything to One's self? The little One would make of One's self by concentrating on It to the exclusion of everything else would still be vastly greater than anything One could make of Itself lost amidst the unimaginably vast and complex everything utterly engulfing It. Just imagine all the potential for realizing a more meaningful life One would waste by choosing to play the unimaginably small and insignificant part in it all you propose One play. Talk about selling One's self short.

O: Nothing like as short as One would sell Itself if It played at living the life you're advocating. There's more to One that just Its One-sidedness. Or there could be. One has within Itself to be profoundly aware of being with a great many other things with beings of their own. To cater utterly to One's selfish side is to take a being with the powers to live a deep, well-rounded life in the company of a great variety of other existing things and make nothing at all of It in comparison to what It could have been. It is to take a being with the capacities to know Itself to be profoundly part of something far greater and deeper than Itself alone and make of It an utterly flat and predictable bore, if not a complete simpleton.

T: It is also to make One's life as simple and straightforward as possible, instead of as confusing and difficult as possible.

O: No, it's not—because life can't be as simple as that. It can't be all about One's self. Not even just apparently, because One is not all there is to One's power to be and mean. There's a whole world of other things, including other Ones, involved in One's power to realize life and more besides—things One can ill-afford to be disrespectful of, if Its life means anything at all to It. Which is why you weren't entirely right when you said that making the most of One's life is simply a matter of getting all One possibly can out of the world and Its life for as little cost to One's own self as possible. You should have said "for as little cost to everything as possible." The trick to making the most of One's life is to make the most One can of the potential for more It shares with the rest of the world while depleting that potential as little as possible, so as to leave as much as possible for as many others as possible to use in doing the same.

T: But that's ridiculous. How is One to do that? It can't keep the whole world in mind at once. In fact, It can keep almost nothing at all in mind at once compared to how much there is to know about at any one instant. And what with everything changing all at once all the time as it does, everything's different from one instant to the next.

O: I didn't say it was going to be easy.

T: Or possible.

O: Oh, it's possible all right. It's even possible for One to do the best It can at making the most of Its life. It's just not possible for One to do it alone. Though it's true that all any One can know of everything is but a very, very small part, One need not face the overwhelming darkness of Its imposed ignorance alone. Not if It can trust enough other Ones to watch out for It as well as themselves. Indeed, how justified any One is in believing Itself to have the power to realize a most meaningful life depends on how much It can believe in those around It, how much It can trust them to treat with deep respect the potential they all share for making Everything of everything. One who is united with every One else around It not only in the belief in every One's right to a good and gainful life, but also in the acknowledgement of the deep dependence of every One on every One and everything else for the deeply real power to realize such a life—such a right—is One who has deeply real reason in the form of others for believing in Its power to make a profoundly meaningful difference in the world and in Its own life. One whose belief in Itself is so justified is One who may know the world to be less overwhelmingly huge and complex than wonderfully mysterious. It is One who may even know a most profound sense of wonder that It is at all, deep in the midst of it all, playing Its meaningful part in the greatest Mystery of all.

T: That you can even envision such a world suggests to us that you weren't so much thinking as you were dreaming, after all. Only One who was dreaming could see such a world as that as possible.

O: Just because it can't and won't happen like a dream doesn't mean it's impossible.

T: To most Ones it does. How else explain the obsession with getting ever more for ever less? The mad fascination with ease and the cost-free speed with which it enables One to do things?

O: There's nothing easy about the lives we're living because of it.

T: Still, ease is all it's all about. Or at least realizing the means to make the realization of One's every dream happen just like a dream.

O: It might look like it's about that, but I don't know that it really is. I know we are forever showing and telling ourselves of the endless more for endless less on our parts we can have by means of more and more ever-more powerful tools. I also know that sharing no end of such information amongst ourselves has done much to make us mad enough for all that more, as well as our tools, to give our lives for both. But our lives don't seem to be growing any more meaningful for all the life we put into realizing the means to make them so. For sure they're not growing any easier. Instead, we seem to be working like mad to realize the means to save life we don't have time to live in any case. It's as though we've gone from believing in the importance of using our tools to make more of our lives to using our lives to make more of our tools. Or from believing in the importance of using our powers to know and dream and realize dreams to make more of the world and our lives to believing no One should ever have been in the first place. Only tools should have been that were as indifferent to their own existence as the world in which they resided.

T: Well, in light of the vast difference between the power One wields in Its dreams and the powers It has to realize Its dreams, it's no wonder One's life makes no sense at all. The only reason One can dream, it seems, is to show Itself how very little reason It really has for being.

O: That's ridiculous.

T: Isn't that what I just said?

O: No. I don't mean One's life is ridiculous. I mean what you said is ridiculous. Only One who couldn't dream of any but the most ridiculous things to do with Its life could believe such nonsense as that. How great the difference is between the power

One has in Its dreams and the power It has in the real world depends on how realistic One's dreams are—how closely they mirror the deep reality of One's being. One who dreams with too little thought to the way things really deeply are is One who can hardly expect reality to side with It in any of Its endeavours to realize Its dreams.

Of course, how realistic One's dreams are is bound to depend on how true to deep reality is the information with which One makes up Its mind about things. If considerable liberties are taken with such information before ever that information is passed on to One—if the information One depends on for knowledge of the possibilities inherent in Its being deep in the midst of everything is so processed and distorted by the time It reaches One that it barely resembles the original information on which it is based; if it is no longer information derived from the direct exchange of being with other deeply real things but "dreamed up" information instead—then it is going to do little, if anything, to help One dream up reasonable dreams to live by. Awareness raised on nonsense can do no One any real good.

Information cannot only enlighten and empower One, it can also blind and overpower One. Just look at how money can deceive and demean One. Not only can money be made to intervene in every exchange any One could possibly have with the world without and about It, it can also be made to appear to be of much more value than the things from which it derives its value by the extreme speed with which the usefulness of such things is driven out of every One's mind by every One's frantic efforts to sell as much as fast as possible and make as much money as fast as possible. Every One may believe Itself to be engaged in the pursuit of the most power to make the most of life, but what Its life is really about is the pursuit of an endless stream of meaningless, pure numbers. It is purely for the sake of the shear quantity of money It might go through in life that One is really living.

The means to realize all manner of worldly things and events out of nothing more than the information that superficially describes them to One can empower One to encounter far more such things in Its life than It ever could through Its own firsthand experience. All the same, One can still take in only so much so fast. Speed, then, is not the answer, any more than the vast quantities it avails One of. Not the whole answer, certainly. Indeed, an utter obeisance to speed reduces everything it lets fly through the mind of One to a seemingly endless stream of meaningless things, by spreading the limited capacity of One's mind so thinly over everything that One can never really be mindful of anything, let alone understand how such a thing might come to be and what might come of it in turn. And One who doesn't really understand anything doesn't know how to make more of the potential It so deeply shares with the rest of the world, let alone how to make the most of It.

The information we Ones glean from our direct and indirect exchanges of being with One another and the rest of the world cannot only give us the know-how to survive in the world. It can also empower us to know enough to dream of more to believe we are for than simply to exist. Or the medium for the exchange of being can lead us so far into the superficial worlds of our dreams that we can no longer find our way in the deeply real world. It is up to us what we make of the information we glean from the experience of being deep in the midst of everything. It is up to us whether we use it to ask too little or too much of ourselves and the world roundabout us, or enough of ourselves to really make something—maybe even Everything—of the potential for more we share with One another and the rest of the world. We will get what we pay for, and that includes what we pay the most attention to. If that be dreams so little based on the reality of our deeply shared being as to be the source of but little, if any, deeply real power to impart meaning to our lives, then our lives and our dreams will never amount to anything more than mere dreams—dreams that will vanish with us, just as any merely apparent thing does when there is no longer the embodied presence of mind to pay it any heed. All that remains of such a thing then is the stuff on which it is described, a stuff that really has nothing but Nothing to do with it.

Any meaning any form of information has for One it has only by virtue of the differences other fully embodied things can make in One's life and One in their beings. It is such things that information is about. Which is why information loses its power to empower One to make more of Its life when it drifts too free of its roots in the deep reality of One's being. When it does, causes become disconnected from effects, means from ends, and costs become lost to view taking with them any value they might have accrued, and all becomes meaningless. All is for naught.

Thus, even as it becomes easier and easier for One to seem to forsake the old, ungainly material world for the new, sleek and supple worlds of information, One must take care to remain sufficiently mindful of the former. It must take care to maintain a deep appreciation for the root source of Its powers to be and mean here. And of course, by One is meant every One. For no One can survive and realize a meaningful life entirely on Its own. No One's powers to be and realize deep meaning in being are Its alone. They are powers shared by all. Which is why it matters so much what we Ones show and tell ourselves about ourselves and the world without and about us all—the information we share with One another. We cannot choose wisely how to make the most of the worldly potential we all share for being and meaning without knowing what we need to know to do so—without being sufficiently aware of the profoundly important role we and the rest of the world play in One another's life. Whether we like it or not, it matters what we see, what we know and believe, because It matters how we behave in the world and we behave in accordance with what we know and believe to be true. And such will continue to matter so long as no One can live on dreams alone—so long as no One can, in fact, realize something out of nothing. So long as we are so deeply dependent on the world without, about and throughout us all for our lives and everything in them, how we behave in that world will matter deeply. One's truth will require material proof and One's values substance. Mere appearances alone cannot be enough—let alone everything. There must be substance behind appearances to back them up before we can allow them to carry much weight with us.

T: My but you do go on, don't you, when given half a chance? Talk about overwhelming One with information—or Nine rather—with meaningless, "dreamed-up" information too. Like I said, you must be dreaming to see any such world as that as possible.

O: Of course I am. That's what dreams are for—greater things to be for than simply are or will be.

T: Well, for sure there's nothing even remotely simple about the world you're dreaming of. Do you have any idea how many Ones it would take to realize a world like that? A whole lot more than just you.

O: One can't realize such a world alone, I admit. But One cannot live in such a world without doing Its part either.

T: But if no One else is going to do Its part, why do One's own? What would be the point?

O: The same point—or reason—a good many other Ones might well consider doing their respective parts. It's all we Ones can do, if we really want to make the most of our world and our lives. In a sense, then, my dream is less a dream than a reality. At least part of it is. The part about what we have to do—stay awake to and careful of the deeply real source of our power to realize meaningful lives.

T: Instead of losing yourselves in your dreams.

O: Well, no One can live on dreams alone—any more than any One can on words, pictures and numbers alone. One who finds it hard to believe that should try writing the words "air sufficient to breath for an hour" on a piece of paper and put that paper and Its head in a plastic bag and close off the end, so no more deeply real air can get in for at least an hour.

T: I could do that no problem.

O: With a big enough plastic bag, no doubt.

T: Just big enough to squeeze my head into would be all I'd need.

O: To still be here after an hour's time?

T: All Two of me, yes—as here as I ever was.

O: But that's ridiculous—unless you're not even what you look to be. Unless you've been trying to get me to see there's more to you than I can see, when in fact there's less to you than I can see.

T: Whatever do you mean by that?

[*Behind a Two posed in puzzlement, Three breaks into a smile of satisfaction and Four bends to stare fixedly at One.*]

O: Like you already said—twice in fact—I must be dreaming to believe I can see what I'm seeing. Only a dream of a being could take its life and save it too—a being such as you, Two.

Behind a Two posed in puzzlement, Three breaks into a smile of satisfaction and Four bends to stare fixedly at One.

I should have known. And I did, though I wasn't altogether conscious of knowing. It's why I've never been especially upset about being here in the midst of all this Nothing. I can afford not to be, because I don't really have to be in the midst of it. I still have everything to live for. I'm only dreaming I don't. And now I can see you're really nothing but Nothing to me, I can see right through all Nine of you. You talk big, but that's all you are—talk. At least it's all *you* are, Two. Three and Four aren't even that it seems. The Two of you talk of a life easier and fuller than any meaningful life could possibly be. But then words are cheap. Or at least they can be. And yours certainly are, Two—too cheap for words even. Meaning costs, deep meaning especially. In deep reality there is no such thing as free power, free value or freedom that is free. There is more to being powerful than doing everything with absolute ease and more to being free than getting everything free, because there is more to more than simply something for nothing. There is something that *can* be, and only if some One gives enough of Itself to the appreciation of the things involved in making it possible.

T: You're hardly One to talk about appreciation. Judging from your treatment of us, you know nothing about any such thing. Even after all we just did for you—going so much out of our way as we did to help you make Ten in spite of yourself. We were supposed to just let you be from here on out.

O: It'll take a lot more than just the three of the Nine of you to empower me to make more of myself. You're just figments—or figures—of my imagination. Ghosts. It's typical of ghosts to jump out at One from nowhere and nothing at all, as you've done with me. Me, though, I've no more time for ghosts. Making the most of One's life involves knowing when too little is too little and too much is too much—when enough is enough, in other words. And I think I've had quite enough of the Two of the Nine of you.

T: Look who's talking big now. As though you were any more than talk yourself.

O: I am—whatever I do—because, unlike you, I'm real through and through. The things that describe me don't just describe me. They are me, and I am them. So I cannot help but make a difference in the world. However, I can help—to some degree at least—what sort of difference I make. And I don't want to it to be the sort of difference you're suggesting I make for you. For that's who or what I would be making it for. I would be acting on your behalf, not mine, if I took your advice and followed it. I would be empowering you to make a difference in the world through me, thereby giving you a sort of deep reality. But I have no intention of making myself as dependent as you are on the actions of things outside myself for my power to be and mean. You're nothing but a dream, and as such, you need to be perceived by the likes of me before you can even merely appear to be. Which does mean you don't have to wait around until some One comes along and pays you the mind you need to be at all. Me, though, I have to put in my time. Every moment of It, for as long as I am. And I don't intend to waste any more of It on the nonsensical likes of you.

T: [*For once Two is as speechless as Three and Four.*]

O: [*Thinks a moment.*] Perhaps I'm being too hard on you. Perhaps I do owe you something. After all, you have made me stop and think about a lot of material things, material in both the physical and the significant sense. Thanks to you, I can now better see that the potential for more is here within everything. It's just up to us to realize it. It's also up to us to realize that it is not how limited and costly our powers for being are that will cause us to make little or nothing of the world and ourselves, but what we do with the powers we have. Or in other words, it is not what we have, but what we do with what we have that will make all the difference in the world and in our lives. That much you have shown me—everything and more.

To show my gratitude for what I have learned with you, I will share it with you one more time before I, for a change, take my leave of you, instead of you of me.

From what we Ones perceive of being deep in the midst of everything,
we dream of more to believe we are for
than to merely persist in being.
Then we give of ourselves to realize that more,
that more than simply all there is,
that everything and more might actually exist

and prove our dreams to be the means
by which greater things might be
than can be seen by simply seeing
what is simply there to see...
...So long as we do not deceive ourselves
into trusting wholly in our dreams
to empower us to realize the greatest of all beings.
For our dreams are but a part
of the power that is ours
to make light of the dark
that haunts our waking hours
with the Mystery of why we are
and have such daunting power.

Alas,
there are more ways than one for One to be without.
Not only could One be without the wherewithal
to do the things It dreams about,
One could also be with all the wherewithal
to realize Its every dream
without ever giving aught at all
to all that It can mean.
Either way One would await outside of everything
without a means of entry into meaning anything.

The stuff of dreams is but the stuff of dreams
if its meaning go no deeper
than the superficial world
in the mind of One lone dreamer.
Words, numbers and pictures
that mean nothing more than Naught
to One who has the means
of leaving dreams
for things deeper than mere thought.
Having left to be with Nothing
and become Its Everything,
One could dream of doing nothing
but recalling everything.

And yet all has not returned It
to where It was before
all became words, numbers, and pictures
and very little more.
How else is One to leave, then,
the seeming leaving that It took
but with the greatest ease and speed
by simply closing up the book? . . .